EXPERIENCE PUERTO RICO: A TRAVEL PREPARATION GUIDE

DELZY HAMPTON

TABLE OF CONTENTS

INTRODUCTION

Puerto Rico is a beautiful Caribbean island with a rich history and culture. It is a popular tourist destination, known for its beaches, resorts, and outdoor activities. However, there is much more to Puerto Rico than just its beaches. There are also many historical sites, museums, and other attractions to explore.

This travel guide will help you plan your trip to Puerto Rico. It will provide you with information on everything from where to stay and what to eat to what to see and do. The guide is divided into several sections, each of which covers a different aspect of Puerto Rico.

Getting to Puerto Rico

The most common way to get to Puerto Rico is by plane. There are several airlines that offer direct flights from major cities in the United States. Once you arrive in Puerto Rico, you can either rent a car or take a taxi to your hotel.

Where to Stay

There are many different hotels in Puerto Rico, to suit all budgets. If you are looking for a beachfront resort, there are many options to choose from. If you are on a budget, there are also many affordable hotels in the city.

What to Eat

Puerto Rican cuisine is a blend of Spanish, African, and Caribbean influences. There are many delicious dishes to try, including mofongo, pastelón, and coquito.

What to See and Do

There are many things to see and do in Puerto Rico. Some of the most popular attractions include:

- **Old San Juan:** The historic walled city of Old San Juan is a UNESCO World Heritage Site. It is home to many historical buildings, including the Castillo San Felipe del Morro, the Catedral Basilica Menor de San Juan Bautista, and the Casa Blanca.

- **Old San Juan in Puerto RicoEl Yunque National Forest:** El Yunque is the only tropical rainforest in the US National Forest System. It is home to a variety of plants and animals, including the coquí frog, the national symbol of Puerto Rico.
- **El Yunque National Forest in Puerto RicoCondado:** Condado is a popular beach resort area. It is home to many hotels, restaurants, and shops.
- **Condado in Puerto RicoVieques:** Vieques is a small island off the coast of Puerto Rico. It is known for its beautiful beaches, bioluminescent bays, and undeveloped nature.
- **Vieques in Puerto RicoCulebra:** Culebra is another small island off the coast of Puerto Rico. It is known for its beautiful beaches, laid-back atmosphere, and snorkeling and diving opportunities.

Planning Your Trip

When planning your trip to Puerto Rico, it is important to consider the time of year. The best time to visit is during the winter, when the weather is warm and sunny. However, the island is also a popular destination during the summer, when the weather is hot and humid.

It is also important to book your accommodations and flights in advance, especially if you are traveling during the peak season.

Puerto Rico is a beautiful and diverse island with something to offer everyone. With its rich history, culture, and natural beauty, Puerto Rico is a great place to visit for a relaxing vacation or an adventurous getaway.

I hope this travel guide has helped you plan your trip to Puerto Rico.

GEOGRAPHY AND CLIMATE

Puerto Rico, officially known as the Commonwealth of Puerto Rico, is an unincorporated territory of the United States located in the northeastern Caribbean Sea. It is the smallest of the Greater Antilles and is composed of the main island of Puerto Rico and several smaller islands and islets. The geography and climate of Puerto Rico are diverse, with a combination of mountainous terrain, coastal areas, and tropical climate.

Geography:

Puerto Rico's geography is characterized by its mountainous interior, low-lying coastal plains, and numerous rivers. The island is approximately 100 miles long and 35 miles wide, with a total land area of about 3,515 square miles. The Cordillera Central, a mountain range running across the central part of the island, is the dominant feature of Puerto Rico's topography. It includes the highest peak, Cerro de Punta, which reaches an elevation of 4,390 feet (1,338 meters) above sea level.

The coastal plains of Puerto Rico are mostly located along the northern and southern coasts.

The northern coastal plain is wider and more developed, hosting major cities such as San Juan, while the southern coastal plain is narrower and less populated. The island is surrounded by beautiful beaches, with the northeastern coast being particularly known for its white sandy shores.

In addition to the main island, Puerto Rico also consists of several smaller islands and islets. The largest of these is Vieques, located east of the main island, followed by Culebra, located to the northeast. These islands offer stunning natural beauty, including pristine beaches, coral reefs, and diverse marine life.

Natural Resources:

Puerto Rico possesses various natural resources, both on land and in its surrounding waters. The island has fertile soils that support agriculture, particularly the cultivation of sugar cane, coffee, bananas, and tobacco. However, due to urbanization and industrial development, agricultural activities have declined over the years.

The surrounding waters of Puerto Rico are rich in marine resources. Fishing is an important economic activity, providing sustenance and livelihoods for many communities. The coastal areas are also home to coral reefs, which support a wide array of marine biodiversity.

Furthermore, Puerto Rico has mineral resources such as copper, nickel, and gold, although their extraction has been limited due to environmental concerns and economic factors. The island has also made efforts to harness renewable energy sources, including solar and wind power, to reduce dependence on fossil fuels.

Climate:

Puerto Rico has a tropical climate characterized by warm temperatures throughout the year and distinct wet and dry seasons. The climate is influenced by its location in the Caribbean Sea and the trade winds that blow from the east.

The average annual temperature in Puerto Rico ranges from 75 to 85 degrees Fahrenheit (24 to 29 degrees Celsius), with relatively small seasonal variations. The coastal areas experience cooler temperatures due to the sea breezes, while the inland areas are slightly warmer.

The rainy season in Puerto Rico typically occurs from May to November, coinciding with the Atlantic hurricane season. During this period, the island receives the majority of its annual rainfall, with the mountainous regions experiencing higher precipitation than the coastal areas. The southern coast, particularly the region around Ponce, tends to be drier compared to the rest of the island.

Hurricanes are a common occurrence in Puerto Rico, with the island being susceptible to their impacts. Major hurricanes, such as Hurricane Maria in 2017, have caused significant damage to infrastructure and natural resources.

HISTORY AND CULTURE

Puerto Rico, a vibrant archipelago located in the northeastern Caribbean, boasts a captivating history and a diverse cultural tapestry that has evolved over centuries. Influenced by indigenous

Taíno tribes, Spanish colonization, African heritage, and American influence, Puerto Rico's history and culture are a captivating blend of traditions, customs, and resilience. This section aims to explore the rich historical and cultural heritage of Puerto Rico, highlighting key events, influences, and iconic aspects that shape the island's identity.

Pre-Columbian Era:

Before the arrival of European explorers, the Taíno people inhabited Puerto Rico. They established agricultural societies, developed complex political systems, and crafted intricate art and pottery. Taíno influences can still be seen in Puerto Rican cuisine, vocabulary, and the island's symbolic coquí frog.

Spanish Colonization:

In 1493, Christopher Columbus arrived in Puerto Rico during his second voyage to the New World. The island soon became a Spanish colony, known as "La Isla de San Juan Bautista." Spanish colonization profoundly impacted Puerto Rico's language, religion, architecture, and governance. Spanish forts, such as El Morro and San Cristóbal, still stand today as UNESCO World Heritage Sites.

African Heritage and Slavery:

The transatlantic slave trade brought African captives to Puerto Rico, who played a significant role in shaping the island's culture. African traditions, music, dance, and cuisine infused with Spanish and indigenous elements, creating vibrant art forms like bomba and plena. Afro-Puerto Rican culture continues to thrive and is celebrated during festivals and cultural events.

U.S. Rule and American Influence:

After the Spanish-American War in 1898, Puerto Rico became a territory of the United States. American influence brought economic changes, industrialization, and infrastructure development to the island. The blending of Puerto Rican and American cultures gave rise to unique phenomena, such as the emergence of Puerto Rican literature and art influenced by both cultures.

National Identity and Autonomy:

Throughout the 20th century, Puerto Rico experienced debates and movements regarding its political status. While Puerto Ricans are U.S.

citizens, the island's relationship with the United States continues to evolve. The discussion of statehood, independence, or maintaining the current commonwealth status shapes the island's political landscape and national identity.

Folklore, Music, and Dance:

Puerto Rican folklore, music, and dance are integral parts of the island's cultural fabric. Bomba, plena, and salsa are lively musical genres that express the history, joys, and struggles of the Puerto Rican people. Traditional dances, such as the salsa-influenced "bomba" and the lively "bomba plena," reflect the island's multi-ethnic heritage.

Gastronomy:

Puerto Rican cuisine is a fusion of Taíno, Spanish, African, and American culinary influences. Iconic dishes like arroz con gandules (rice with pigeon peas), mofongo (mashed plantains), and lechón (roast pig) represent the island's rich gastronomic tradition. The vibrant flavors and diverse ingredients make Puerto Rican cuisine a delight for food enthusiasts.

Art, Literature, and Architecture:

The artistic expression of Puerto Rico is a reflection of its history and cultural identity. Renowned artists like Francisco Oller and Rafael Tufiño have left a lasting impact on Puerto Rican art, while writers like Julia de Burgos and Esmeralda Santiago have contributed significantly to Puerto Rican literature. Architecture in Puerto Rico showcases a blend of Spanish colonial, neoclassical, and modernist styles.

Puerto Rico's history and culture are a testament to the resilience and creativity of its people. The blending of indigenous, Spanish, African, and American influences has shaped the island's vibrant heritage. From its pre-Columbian roots to Spanish colonization, African heritage, and the complexities of U.S. rule, Puerto Rico's history is rich and multifaceted. Its folklore, music, cuisine, and artistic expressions reflect the island's diverse cultural tapestry. As Puerto Rico continues to navigate its political status, its history and culture remain essential elements in defining its unique identity.

CHAPTER ONE

PLANNING YOUR TRIP

Planning a trip to Puerto Rico promises an unforgettable experience filled with captivating landscapes, rich history, vibrant culture, and warm hospitality. As you embark on this adventure, meticulous planning will ensure you make the most of your time on this enchanting Caribbean island. This comprehensive guide provides a detailed overview of Puerto Rico, including transportation options, accommodation recommendations, popular attractions, gastronomic delights, and practical travel tips. By following this guide, you'll be well-equipped to create a memorable and seamless trip to Puerto Rico.

Getting There:
a. Flight options: Explore the availability of direct flights to Puerto Rico from your location, taking into account major airlines and travel aggregators.

b. Airports: Determine which airport to fly into, with San Juan's Luis Muñoz Marín International Airport being the primary gateway.

c. Visa and documentation: Verify the passport and visa requirements based on your nationality and duration of stay.

1. **d. Transportation:** Research transportation options from the airport to your accommodation, including taxis, ride-sharing services, public buses, and car rentals.

Accommodation:

a. Types of accommodation: Choose from a range of options, such as luxury resorts, boutique hotels, budget-friendly guesthouses, or vacation rentals.

b. Popular regions: Explore the different regions of Puerto Rico, including San Juan, Old San Juan, Condado, Isla Verde, and Rincón, to identify the ideal location for your stay.

2. **c. Booking platforms:** Utilize reputable booking platforms and read reviews to find the perfect accommodation that suits your preferences and budget.

Attractions and Activities:

a. Old San Juan: Discover the charm of the historic district, including iconic landmarks like El Morro Fortress and Castillo de San Cristóbal.

b. El Yunque National Forest: Explore the lush rainforest with its scenic trails, waterfalls, and diverse flora and fauna.

c. Culebra and Vieques Islands: Consider a day trip to these stunning islands, renowned for pristine beaches and snorkeling opportunities.

d. Bioluminescent Bay: Experience the magic of Mosquito Bay in Vieques or Laguna Grande in Fajardo, where the water glows with bioluminescent organisms.

e. Ponce: Visit the southern city known for its vibrant art scene, impressive architecture, and the iconic Ponce Museum of Art.

3. **f. Outdoor adventures:** Engage in thrilling activities such as ziplining, kayaking, hiking, and surfing in various locations across the island.

Cultural Experiences:
a. Local festivals and events: Check the calendar for festivals like the San Sebastián Street Festival, Casals Festival, and the Puerto Rico Salsa

Congress, offering a glimpse into the island's rich cultural heritage.

b. Food and drink: Indulge in Puerto Rico's gastronomic delights, such as mofongo, lechón, arroz con gandules, and refreshing tropical drinks like piña colada and coquito.

4. **c. Music and dance:** Immerse yourself in the rhythms of salsa, reggaeton, and bomba, and learn to dance at a local salsa club or take a dance lesson.

Practical Considerations:

a. Language and currency: English and Spanish are widely spoken, and the official currency is the US dollar.

b. Safety: Familiarize yourself with safety guidelines and precautions, including avoiding isolated areas and practicing common-sense precautions.

c. Weather and packing: Research the weather conditions during your travel dates and pack accordingly, considering lightweight clothing, comfortable footwear, and sunscreen.

d. Health and travel insurance: Check if any vaccinations are required and consider travel insurance to protect against unforeseen circumstances.

5. **e. Local customs and etiquette:** Familiarize yourself with local customs, such as greetings, tipping practices, and respectful behavior.

BEST TIME TO VISIT

Puerto Rico, a vibrant island located in the Caribbean, offers a diverse range of attractions, from stunning beaches and lush rainforests to historical sites and a vibrant culture. To make the most of your visit to this enchanting destination, it is important to consider the best time to experience the various wonders it has to offer. This guide will delve into the climate, festivals, and tourist seasons to help you determine the optimal time to plan your trip to Puerto Rico.

Climate Overview:

1. Puerto Rico enjoys a tropical climate, characterized by year-round warmth and high humidity. The island experiences two distinct seasons: the dry season (winter) and the wet season (summer). However, it is worth noting that Puerto Rico is a popular destination all year round due to its pleasant temperatures and constant trade winds.

Dry Season (December to April):

2. The dry season is considered the peak tourist season in Puerto Rico due to the favorable weather conditions. With average temperatures ranging from 70°F (21°C) to 85°F (29°C), visitors can enjoy outdoor activities, beach excursions, and exploration of the island's natural beauty. Moreover, this period aligns with the winter months in North America, making it an appealing escape from colder climates. It is important to note that prices tend to be higher during this season, and popular attractions may be more crowded.

Wet Season (May to November):

3. The wet season in Puerto Rico is characterized by higher humidity, occasional rain showers, and the potential for tropical storms and hurricanes. While this might deter some tourists, it also brings several advantages. The prices of accommodations and flights are generally lower during this period, and you may find fewer crowds at popular tourist sites. Additionally, if you plan your visit during the early months of the wet season, such as May or June, you can still enjoy pleasant weather with intermittent rain showers.

Festivals and Events:

4. One of the most captivating aspects of Puerto Rico is its vibrant festival calendar, filled with cultural celebrations and events that showcase the island's rich heritage. Some of the notable festivals include the San Sebastián Street Festival in January, the Ponce Carnival in February, and the Casals Festival in March. Attending these festivities adds a unique and immersive experience to your visit, and it is worth considering the

timing of these events when planning your trip.

Off-Peak Travel Seasons:

5. If you prefer to avoid large crowds and are looking for more affordable travel options, the shoulder seasons of spring and autumn are excellent alternatives. From mid-April to May and from September to November, Puerto Rico experiences lower visitor numbers, making it an ideal time for a peaceful vacation. During these months, you can still enjoy pleasant temperatures, although there might be a higher chance of rain showers.

Specific Activities and Interests:

6. The best time to visit Puerto Rico may also depend on your specific interests and activities you plan to engage in during your trip. For example, surfers may prefer the months of December to March when the Atlantic swells are at their peak. Nature enthusiasts might enjoy visiting El Yunque National Forest during the wet season when

the lush greenery is at its most vibrant. Snorkeling and diving enthusiasts may find the summer months ideal for exploring the crystal-clear waters around the island.

Determining the best time to visit Puerto Rico requires considering various factors, such as weather preferences, festival dates, and personal interests. While the dry season from December to April is the peak tourist season, offering the most reliable weather, the wet season from May to November can provide unique advantages such as lower prices and fewer crowds. Ultimately, the choice depends on your individual preferences and priorities. With its year-round warm climate and diverse attractions, Puerto Rico has something to offer for every traveler, regardless of the time of year.

ENTRY REQUIREMENTS AND VISA INFORMATION

If you are planning to travel to Puerto Rico, it is important to familiarize yourself with the entry requirements and visa information to ensure a smooth and hassle-free journey. In this section, we will explore the entry requirements and visa regulations for visiting Puerto Rico.

Visa Waiver Program:

One of the key advantages for travelers visiting Puerto Rico is that it falls under the Visa Waiver Program (VWP). The VWP allows citizens of certain countries to travel to the United States, including Puerto Rico, for tourism or business purposes without obtaining a visa. Travelers under the VWP are eligible for a 90-day stay, and their purpose of travel must not involve employment or study. It is essential to note that although Puerto Rico is part of the United States, it has its own specific regulations for entry.

Passport Requirements:

To enter Puerto Rico, all travelers must possess a valid passport. The passport should be valid for at least six months beyond the intended departure date from Puerto Rico. It is advisable to check the expiration date of your passport well in advance and renew it if necessary to avoid any complications during your travel.

ESTA Authorization:

If you are traveling to Puerto Rico under the VWP, you will need to apply for Electronic System for Travel Authorization (ESTA) authorization before your trip. ESTA is an online application system administered by the United States Department of Homeland Security. It determines the eligibility of visitors to travel to Puerto Rico (and other parts of the United States) without a visa. The ESTA application must be completed at least 72 hours before departure. Upon approval, the ESTA authorization is valid for multiple entries within a two-year period or until the expiration of your passport, whichever comes first.

Visa Requirements:

If you are not eligible for the Visa Waiver Program or if your intended stay in Puerto Rico exceeds 90 days, you will need to obtain a nonimmigrant visa. The most common nonimmigrant visa category for tourist or business purposes is the B-1/B-2 visa. To apply for a B-1/B-2 visa, you will need to schedule an appointment at the nearest U.S. embassy or consulate and submit the required documentation, including a completed visa application form, a valid passport, a photograph, proof of financial resources, and evidence of ties to your home country. The visa application process can vary in duration, so it is advisable to apply well in advance of your planned travel dates.

Transit through the United States:

If you are transiting through the United States to reach Puerto Rico, you may need to obtain a transit visa, depending on your nationality. Transit visa requirements vary, so it is important to check with the U.S. embassy or consulate in your home country to determine whether you need a transit visa for your specific travel itinerary.

Extension of Stay:

If you are in Puerto Rico under the Visa Waiver Program and wish to extend your stay beyond the initial 90 days, it is generally not possible. The VWP does not allow for extensions. If you need to stay longer, you will have to leave Puerto Rico and reenter after a significant period of time has passed.

Additional Considerations:

While visiting Puerto Rico, it is important to remember that local laws and regulations apply. It is advisable to familiarize yourself with Puerto Rico's customs and immigration policies to ensure compliance during your stay. In addition, it is recommended to have travel insurance that covers medical expenses, as healthcare in Puerto Rico can be costly for visitors without insurance.

By understanding the entry requirements and visa information, you can ensure a smooth and enjoyable journey. Whether you are eligible for the Visa Waiver Program or need to obtain a nonimmigrant visa, make sure to plan ahead, check the validity of your passport, and fulfill all necessary documentation requirements. By doing so, you can embark on your Puerto Rican adventure with peace of mind and a clear understanding of the entry regulations.

GETTING TO PUERTO RICO

Puerto Rico, a tropical paradise located in the Caribbean, offers an enticing blend of natural beauty, vibrant culture, and historical significance. Whether you're planning a leisurely vacation or considering relocating to this U.S. territory, understanding the various ways of getting into Puerto Rico is essential. This comprehensive guide will delve into the numerous travel options available, including air travel, cruises, and ferry services, as well as discuss the documentation requirements for entry into the island. By the end, you will have a solid understanding of how to embark on an unforgettable journey to Puerto Rico.

Air Travel

1. One of the most popular and convenient ways to reach Puerto Rico is by air travel.

With several major airports serving the island, visitors have numerous options to choose from. The primary airport is the Luis Muñoz Marín International Airport (SJU) located near San Juan, which connects Puerto Rico to various destinations around the world. Additionally, other regional airports such as Rafael Hernández Airport (BQN) in Aguadilla and Mercedita International Airport (PSE) in Ponce offer alternative entry points.

Cruise Ships

2. Another exciting option for traveling to Puerto Rico is by embarking on a cruise ship. The island serves as a popular port of call for numerous cruise lines, offering visitors a chance to experience Puerto Rico's unique culture while enjoying the amenities and entertainment on board. Major cruise ports in Puerto Rico include the San Juan Cruise Port and the Port of Ponce. These ports welcome thousands of tourists annually, making cruises a convenient and enjoyable way to reach the island.

Ferry Services

3. For those looking to travel to Puerto Rico from neighboring islands or within the archipelago itself, ferry services provide an alternative means of transportation. Ferries operate between Puerto Rico and other Caribbean islands, such as the Dominican Republic and the U.S. Virgin Islands. Additionally, ferry services are available for inter-island travel within Puerto Rico, connecting destinations like San Juan, Vieques, and Culebra. While schedules and availability may vary, ferry services offer a scenic and budget-friendly option for accessing the island.

Documentation Requirements

4. To ensure a smooth entry into Puerto Rico, understanding the documentation requirements is crucial. As a U.S. territory, Puerto Rico follows similar regulations to those for entering the United States. U.S. citizens can enter Puerto Rico with a valid U.S. passport, while non-U.S. citizens must present a valid passport and may require a

visa depending on their country of origin. It is important to review the latest entry requirements and consult with the appropriate authorities to confirm the necessary documentation.

Puerto Rico offers an array of options for travelers seeking to explore its breathtaking landscapes, rich history, and vibrant culture. Whether you choose to arrive by air, cruise ship, or ferry, each mode of transportation provides its unique advantages and experiences. By being aware of the documentation requirements and ensuring you have the necessary paperwork in order, you can confidently embark on your journey to Puerto Rico.

TRANSPORTATION WITHIN PUERTO RICO

Transportation plays a crucial role in the development and connectivity of any region, and

Puerto Rico is no exception. As a Caribbean island with a rich history and diverse cultural heritage, Puerto Rico relies on a robust transportation system to facilitate commerce, tourism, and the movement of people and goods within its borders. In this comprehensive overview, we will delve into the transportation landscape of Puerto Rico, highlighting its various modes of transportation, their historical significance, challenges faced, and notable developments.

Road Transportation:

1. Road transportation serves as the backbone of Puerto Rico's transportation infrastructure. The island has an extensive network of roads and highways that connect its cities, towns, and rural areas. The main highway, Route 52, commonly referred to as the "Luis A. Ferré Expressway," runs from the capital city of San Juan to the southern city of Ponce, facilitating efficient travel between these major urban centers. Puerto Rico's road network is generally well-maintained, offering accessibility and convenience to both residents and tourists.

Public Transportation:

2. **a) Public Buses:** The public bus system, managed by the Metropolitan Bus Authority (AMA), is a primary mode of transportation for many Puerto Ricans. AMA operates a comprehensive network of buses that serve both urban and rural areas, providing affordable and accessible transportation options. However, the bus system has faced challenges with reliability, overcrowding, and limited coverage in some remote regions.

b) Tren Urbano: In an effort to address urban congestion, the Tren Urbano, a rapid transit system, was inaugurated in 2004. The train system connects various municipalities within the San Juan metropolitan area, offering an efficient and eco-friendly alternative to road transportation. Tren Urbano has helped alleviate traffic congestion and reduce travel times for commuters, making it a significant development in Puerto Rico's transportation landscape.

Air Transportation:

3. **a) Luis Muñoz Marín International Airport:**
    As the main international gateway to Puerto
    Rico, the Luis Muñoz Marín International
    Airport, located in San Juan, serves as a
    crucial transportation hub. It offers direct
    flights to major cities in the United States, as
    well as other Caribbean destinations. The
    airport has witnessed steady growth in
    passenger traffic over the years,
    necessitating ongoing infrastructure
    improvements and expansion efforts.

b) Regional Airports: Apart from the international
airport, Puerto Rico has several smaller regional
airports, such as Rafael Hernández Airport in
Aguadilla and Mercedita Airport in Ponce. These
airports serve as vital links for domestic travel and
facilitate inter-island connections. They play a
crucial role in promoting tourism and supporting
economic development in their respective regions.

Maritime Transportation:

4. **a) Ports:** Puerto Rico's strategic location in
    the Caribbean has made it an important
    maritime hub. The Port of San Juan,
    managed by the Puerto Rico Ports Authority,

is the primary seaport on the island. It serves as a vital gateway for both commercial shipping and the cruise industry, contributing significantly to Puerto Rico's economy. The port has undergone modernization initiatives to enhance its capacity and accommodate larger vessels.

b) Ferries: Ferry services operate between Puerto Rico and neighboring islands such as the Dominican Republic, the British Virgin Islands, and the U.S. Virgin Islands. These services provide convenient transportation options for both residents and tourists, fostering regional connectivity and facilitating cultural exchange.

Challenges and Future Developments:

5. Despite the progress made in Puerto Rico's transportation system, several challenges persist. These include inadequate funding for infrastructure maintenance and improvements, traffic congestion in urban areas, limited public transportation coverage in rural regions, and the vulnerability of transportation networks to natural disasters. However, the government and various

stakeholders have recognized these challenges and are actively working on solutions to enhance the island's transportation system.

In recent years, Puerto Rico has made strides towards sustainable transportation, with the promotion of electric vehicles and the integration of renewable energy sources in transportation infrastructure. Additionally, ongoing initiatives focus on improving road networks, expanding public transportation coverage, and incorporating emerging technologies for more efficient transportation management.

Transportation in Puerto Rico encompasses a diverse range of modes that facilitate the movement of people and goods across the island. From the extensive road network to public buses, trains, airports, seaports, and ferries, Puerto Rico's transportation system plays a pivotal role in supporting economic development, promoting tourism, and connecting communities. While challenges persist, ongoing efforts and future developments aim to improve the efficiency, sustainability, and resilience of Puerto Rico's transportation infrastructure, ensuring a brighter future for the island's connectivity and mobility.

ACCOMMODATION OPTIONS

Puerto Rico, a Caribbean island known for its beautiful beaches, rich culture, and vibrant history, offers a wide range of accommodation options for travelers. Whether you're looking for luxury resorts, cozy guesthouses, budget-friendly hotels, or unique vacation rentals, Puerto Rico has something to suit every taste and budget. In this section, we will explore the various accommodation options available on the island.

Luxury Resorts:

1. Puerto Rico boasts several world-class luxury resorts that offer the ultimate in comfort and relaxation. These resorts are often located in stunning beachfront locations and provide a wide range of

amenities and services, including pools, spas, fine dining restaurants, and recreational activities. Some popular luxury resorts in Puerto Rico include The Ritz-Carlton, Dorado Beach, and St. Regis Bahia Beach Resort.

Boutique Hotels:

2. For those seeking a more intimate and personalized experience, boutique hotels are an excellent choice. These smaller, independently owned properties often feature unique designs, stylish décor, and personalized service. Many boutique hotels in Puerto Rico are located in the historic districts of Old San Juan and Ponce, offering easy access to cultural attractions and local landmarks.

Beachfront Hotels:

3. If you're looking to wake up to the sound of crashing waves and enjoy direct beach access, Puerto Rico has a variety of beachfront hotels to choose from. These hotels range from budget-friendly options to

upscale resorts, providing guests with stunning views and convenient access to the island's pristine beaches. Some popular beachfront hotels include Condado Vanderbilt Hotel, Caribe Hilton, and El San Juan Hotel.

Guesthouses and Inns:

4. Guesthouses and inns offer a more intimate and homely atmosphere, often run by local families or individuals. These accommodations are usually smaller in scale, providing personalized service and a chance to connect with the local culture. Many guesthouses and inns in Puerto Rico can be found in charming coastal towns and rural areas, offering a peaceful retreat away from the hustle and bustle of the cities.

Vacation Rentals:

5. For travelers seeking more space and flexibility, vacation rentals are an excellent option. Puerto Rico offers a wide range of vacation rentals, including apartments, condos, villas, and beach houses. These

rentals are equipped with all the necessary amenities for a comfortable stay and often provide a kitchen and living area, allowing guests to have a home-away-from-home experience. Websites such as Airbnb and Vrbo offer a vast selection of vacation rentals across the island.

Eco-Lodges and Nature Retreats:

6. For nature lovers and eco-conscious travelers, Puerto Rico has several eco-lodges and nature retreats that allow visitors to immerse themselves in the island's natural beauty. These accommodations are often situated in lush rainforests or near natural reserves, providing a tranquil environment and opportunities for hiking, birdwatching, and other outdoor activities. Examples of eco-lodges in Puerto Rico include Casa Cubuy Ecolodge and Casa Picaflores.

Paradores:

7. Paradores are a unique type of accommodation found in Puerto Rico, offering a blend of history, culture, and

hospitality. These government-owned inns are typically located in historic buildings, such as former convents, fortresses, or haciendas. Paradores aim to showcase the island's rich heritage while providing comfortable accommodations and traditional Puerto Rican cuisine. Some popular paradores include Parador Combate Beach, Parador Villas Sotomayor, and Parador MaunaCaribe.

Camping and Glamping:

8. For adventurous travelers looking to get closer to nature, Puerto Rico offers camping and glamping opportunities. The island has numerous campgrounds and designated areas for camping, where visitors can pitch tents and enjoy outdoor activities. Additionally, some places provide glamping options, combining the comforts of a hotel with the unique experience of sleeping in nature. Flamenco Beach Eco Glamping in Culebra is a popular glamping site in Puerto Rico.

SAFETY TIPS AND EMERGENCY CONTACTS

Puerto Rico, a vibrant and captivating island in the Caribbean, is known for its beautiful beaches, rich cultural heritage, and warm hospitality. Whether you are a resident or a visitor, it is crucial to prioritize safety to ensure a memorable and incident-free experience on the island. This guide aims to provide comprehensive safety tips and emergency contacts specific to Puerto Rico, helping individuals make informed decisions and handle emergencies effectively.

General Safety Tips

1. **Familiarize Yourself with Local Laws and Customs:** Before traveling to Puerto Rico, take the time to research and understand the local laws, customs, and cultural norms. This will help you avoid unintentional offenses and ensure a respectful experience.
2. **Stay Aware of Your Surroundings:** Regardless of your location, maintaining situational awareness is vital. Be cautious of your surroundings, especially in crowded areas or unfamiliar neighborhoods. Avoid

displaying valuable items openly and keep an eye on your belongings at all times.

3. **Be Mindful of Beach Safety:** Puerto Rico's stunning beaches attract countless visitors each year. However, it is important to exercise caution while swimming. Only swim in designated areas with lifeguards present, pay attention to warning signs, and avoid swimming alone or in adverse weather conditions.

4. **Stay Hydrated and Protect Against the Sun:** Puerto Rico's tropical climate can be intense, particularly during the summer months. Stay hydrated by drinking plenty of water, wear sunscreen, a wide-brimmed hat, and lightweight, breathable clothing to protect yourself from sunburn and heat exhaustion.

5. **Use Reliable Transportation:** When exploring Puerto Rico, ensure you use licensed and reputable transportation services. Taxis and ride-sharing services like Uber are reliable options. If renting a car, be mindful of local traffic laws and road conditions.

Natural Disasters and Weather-Related Safety

1. **Hurricane Preparedness:** Puerto Rico is vulnerable to hurricanes during the Atlantic hurricane season (June to November). Stay informed about weather updates, follow instructions from local authorities, and have a preparedness plan in place. Keep emergency supplies, including food, water, flashlights, batteries, and a first aid kit.
2. **Earthquake Safety:** Puerto Rico is located in an active seismic zone. Familiarize yourself with earthquake safety guidelines, such as "Drop, Cover, and Hold On" during an earthquake. Secure heavy furniture and objects that could become hazards during seismic activity.
3. **Flash Flood Safety:** Heavy rainfall can lead to flash floods in Puerto Rico. Avoid walking or driving through flooded areas, as water levels can rise rapidly and pose a significant risk. Stay informed about weather forecasts and heed warnings from local authorities.

Emergency Contacts

In case of an emergency, it is essential to have access to the appropriate emergency contacts. The following contacts can be helpful in Puerto Rico:

1. Emergency Services:
- Police, Fire, and Medical Emergencies: Dial 911
2. Puerto Rico Tourism Company:
- General Inquiries and Assistance: +1 (787) 721-2400
3. Hospitals and Medical Facilities:
- Centro Médico de Puerto Rico (San Juan): +1 (787) 754-0101
- Hospital Auxilio Mutuo (San Juan): +1 (787) 758-2000
- Hospital San Lucas (Ponce): +1 (787) 844-2080
4. Consulates and Embassies:
- United States Embassy (San Juan): +1 (787) 766-4999
- Embassy of Canada (San Juan): +1 (787) 759-8000
- Embassy of the United Kingdom (San Juan): +1 (787) 721-7989

CHAPTER TWO

SAN JUAN: THE CAPITAL CITY

OVERVIEW OF SAN JUAN

San Juan, the capital city of Puerto Rico, is a vibrant and culturally rich destination that seamlessly blends the charm of its historic past with the modern amenities of a bustling metropolis. With its stunning architecture, cobblestone streets, and colorful colonial buildings, Old San Juan stands as a testament to the city's rich history. Meanwhile, modern San Juan boasts impressive skyscrapers, luxurious resorts, and a thriving nightlife scene. In this section, we will explore the overview of San Juan, with a particular focus on Old San Juan and modern San Juan, highlighting their distinct characteristics and contributions to the city's unique identity.

San Juan is located on the northeastern coast of Puerto Rico and is the island's most populous municipality. Its strategic position in the Caribbean Sea has played a crucial role in its history, making it an important port for trade and military endeavors.

The city was founded by Spanish colonists in 1521 and served as a key stronghold during the era of Spanish colonial rule. Today, San Juan is a captivating blend of Puerto Rican culture and Spanish influences, evident in its architecture, cuisine, and traditions.

Old San Juan, a UNESCO World Heritage Site, is a captivating district that transports visitors back in time. Enclosed by massive stone walls and fortified structures, the district exudes a sense of grandeur and resilience. The blue cobblestone streets and colorful facades of the buildings create a picturesque ambiance that is both charming and captivating. Exploring Old San Juan is like stepping into a living museum, with its well-preserved colonial architecture serving as a reminder of the city's past.

The centerpiece of Old San Juan is the historic fortresses of El Morro and San Cristobal. El Morro, officially known as Castillo San Felipe del Morro, is an imposing citadel perched atop a promontory overlooking the Atlantic Ocean. Constructed in the 16th century, it was designed to protect the city from seaborne invasions. The fortification's towering walls, cannons, and underground tunnels offer visitors a glimpse into the city's military history. San Cristobal, another formidable fortress, guards the eastern entrance to Old San Juan and provides panoramic views of the city and coastline.

Walking through the streets of Old San Juan, visitors will encounter numerous historical landmarks, such as La Fortaleza, the oldest executive mansion in continuous use in the Americas, and the Cathedral of San Juan Bautista, one of the oldest cathedrals in the Western Hemisphere. The narrow streets are lined with boutique shops, art galleries, and quaint cafes, where visitors can immerse themselves in the local culture and indulge in Puerto Rican cuisine, including delicious dishes like mofongo and arroz con gandules.

While Old San Juan celebrates the city's rich history, modern San Juan showcases its cosmopolitan side. The city has undergone significant development in recent decades, with a skyline dominated by sleek high-rise buildings and luxury hotels. The Condado and Isla Verde districts are particularly known for their upscale resorts, pristine beaches, and vibrant nightlife. Here, visitors can enjoy world-class amenities, trendy restaurants, and a lively atmosphere.

Avenida Ashford, in the heart of Condado, is a bustling strip dotted with high-end boutiques, art galleries, and gourmet restaurants. The area also boasts beautiful parks and green spaces, such as the Parque del Indio, where locals and tourists gather to relax and enjoy outdoor activities. Isla Verde, located adjacent to the Luis Muñoz Marín International Airport, offers a stunning beachfront with powdery sand and turquoise waters, attracting sun-seekers and water sports enthusiasts.

For those seeking cultural experiences, modern San Juan has much to offer as well. The Santurce neighborhood is a hub of artistic expression, with its vibrant street art, contemporary galleries, and performance spaces. The Museo de Arte de Puerto Rico showcases a diverse collection of Puerto Rican art, spanning from the 17th century to the present day. The performing arts scene is also thriving in San Juan, with theaters and concert halls hosting a wide range of productions, including plays, concerts, and ballet performances.

San Juan's culinary scene is a reflection of its rich cultural heritage and offers a tantalizing array of flavors and influences. From traditional Puerto Rican cuisine to international fusion, the city caters to all tastes. Local markets, such as La Placita de Santurce, offer a sensory experience, where visitors can sample tropical fruits, fresh seafood, and local delicacies. San Juan is also known for its lively food truck scene, where inventive chefs showcase their culinary skills and serve up mouthwatering dishes.

Beyond its architectural and cultural treasures, San Juan also serves as a gateway to exploring the natural beauty of Puerto Rico. The city's location allows for easy access to stunning beaches, lush rainforests, and other natural wonders. Just a short drive from San Juan, visitors can discover El Yunque National Forest, a tropical paradise known for its waterfalls, hiking trails, and diverse flora and fauna. The nearby islands of Culebra and Vieques offer pristine beaches and world-class snorkeling and diving opportunities.

San Juan is a captivating city that seamlessly combines its historic past with modernity. Old San Juan stands as a testament to the city's rich history, with its well-preserved colonial architecture and historical landmarks. Meanwhile, modern San Juan showcases the city's cosmopolitan side, with its impressive skyline, luxurious resorts, and vibrant nightlife. Together, these two facets of San Juan create a destination that offers a unique blend of cultural immersion, architectural beauty, culinary delights, and natural wonders, making it an enchanting place to visit.

MUSEUMS AND ART GALLERIES

Puerto Rico, a captivating Caribbean island known for its rich history, stunning landscapes, and vibrant culture, is also home to a diverse array of museums and art galleries. These cultural institutions provide visitors with an immersive experience, showcasing the island's artistic heritage and creative expression. In this section, we will delve into the fascinating world of Puerto Rico's museums and art galleries, exploring their historical significance, notable collections, and contributions to the local art scene.

1. **Museo de Arte de Puerto Rico (Museum of Art of Puerto Rico):**

The Museo de Arte de Puerto Rico, located in the Santurce district of San Juan, is a prominent institution that celebrates Puerto Rico's artistic legacy. Established in 2000, this museum houses a vast collection of over 1,000 works spanning various periods and artistic movements. Visitors can explore the galleries to discover indigenous art, colonial-era masterpieces, modern and contemporary artworks, and a range of temporary exhibitions that showcase both local and international talent.

2. **Museo de Arte Contemporáneo de Puerto Rico (Museum of Contemporary Art of Puerto Rico):**

Nestled within the lively Santurce neighborhood, the Museo de Arte Contemporáneo de Puerto Rico is dedicated to promoting and exhibiting contemporary art. Opened in 1984, this museum offers a thought-provoking space for local and international artists to display their creations. Its collection comprises paintings, sculptures, installations, and multimedia artworks that reflect the ever-evolving nature of contemporary artistic expressions.

3. Museo de las Américas (Museum of the Americas):

Situated in Old San Juan, the Museo de las Américas explores the multifaceted heritage and cultural connections of the Americas. This museum chronicles the history of Puerto Rico and its relationship with other regions, showcasing indigenous artifacts, colonial-era objects, and artistic representations that illustrate the diverse narratives of the Americas. It also hosts exhibitions focusing on topics such as African heritage, migration, and social issues, providing visitors with a deeper understanding of Puerto Rico's place in the broader American context.

4. El Museo de la Historia de Ponce (Ponce History Museum):

In the city of Ponce, on Puerto Rico's southern coast, the El Museo de la Historia de Ponce delves into the region's fascinating past. Housed in a grand neoclassical building dating back to 1912, this museum exhibits artifacts, photographs, and documents that trace Ponce's history from its indigenous roots to its colonial period and beyond. It offers a comprehensive exploration of the city's cultural heritage, architecture, and prominent figures, providing valuable insights into the island's history.

5. Museo de Arte de Ponce (Ponce Art Museum):

Renowned for its extensive European and Latin American art collections, the Museo de Arte de Ponce is one of Puerto Rico's most significant art museums. Located in Ponce, this institution boasts an impressive selection of artworks spanning centuries, including paintings, sculptures, and decorative arts. Visitors can marvel at masterpieces by renowned artists such as Velázquez, Rubens, and Rodin, as well as explore the museum's extensive library and educational programs.

6. Caguas Museum of Art:

The Caguas Museum of Art, located in the city of Caguas, showcases Puerto Rico's artistic talent through its diverse exhibitions and cultural events.

This museum places a strong emphasis on contemporary art, featuring works by local artists alongside international contemporary art installations. It offers a space for dialogue and experimentation, encouraging artists to push the boundaries of their creativity and engage with relevant social issues.

Puerto Rico's museums and art galleries are an integral part of the island's cultural fabric, offering visitors a glimpse into its rich artistic heritage and contemporary expressions. From the Museo de Arte de Puerto Rico's comprehensive collection to the Museo de Arte Contemporáneo de Puerto Rico's focus on cutting-edge creations, each institution contributes to the dynamic art scene of Puerto Rico. Whether exploring the historical significance of the Museo de las Américas or immersing oneself in the European masterpieces at the Museo de Arte de Ponce, these cultural institutions provide an enriching and immersive experience for art enthusiasts, historians, and curious visitors alike.

SHOPPING AND ENTERTAINMENT

Puerto Rico, a tropical island located in the Caribbean, is not only known for its stunning beaches and rich cultural heritage but also for its vibrant shopping and entertainment scene. From high-end luxury boutiques to bustling local markets, Puerto Rico offers a diverse range of shopping options that cater to all tastes and budgets. Likewise, the island provides a wide array of entertainment choices, including music, dance, theater, and nightlife, ensuring visitors and residents alike are never short of activities to enjoy. In this section, we will explore the shopping and entertainment experiences that Puerto Rico has to offer.

Shopping in Puerto Rico:

When it comes to shopping, Puerto Rico presents an enticing mix of modern shopping malls, designer boutiques, and traditional marketplaces. San Juan, the capital city, is a shopaholic's paradise, featuring both upscale shopping centers and charming Old San Juan streets lined with unique stores.

One of the must-visit shopping destinations in San Juan is Plaza Las Americas, the largest shopping mall in the Caribbean. With over 300 stores, including renowned international brands and local retailers, Plaza Las Americas offers a diverse range of fashion, electronics, accessories, and more. It also houses various dining options and entertainment facilities, making it a one-stop destination for all your shopping needs.

For those seeking luxury shopping experiences, The Mall of San Juan is an excellent choice. This upscale mall features high-end designer stores such as Louis Vuitton, Gucci, and Jimmy Choo. The Mall of San Juan offers an elegant ambiance and a curated selection of luxury goods, attracting fashion enthusiasts and discerning shoppers.

In addition to these modern shopping malls, Puerto Rico showcases its vibrant local culture through various traditional markets. One such market is the Mercado de Río Piedras, located in the Río Piedras district of San Juan. This lively market offers a wide range of fresh produce, local handicrafts, and traditional food, providing visitors with an authentic Puerto Rican shopping experience.

The Old San Juan streets, characterized by their colorful colonial buildings and cobblestone roads, are another shopping haven. Here, visitors can explore numerous boutique shops offering unique items such as handmade jewelry, art, and locally crafted souvenirs. The bustling streets create an enchanting atmosphere that adds to the charm of the shopping experience.

Beyond San Juan, Puerto Rico offers shopping opportunities throughout the island. Places like Ponce, Mayagüez, and Carolina feature their own shopping centers and local markets, each with its own distinct flavor and offerings. These locations provide visitors with a chance to explore different regions of the island while indulging in retail therapy.

Entertainment in Puerto Rico:

Puerto Rico is renowned for its vibrant and diverse entertainment scene, offering a wide range of cultural, musical, and recreational activities. Music plays a central role in Puerto Rican culture, and visitors have the opportunity to immerse themselves in the island's rhythmic beats through various live performances and festivals.

Salsa, one of the most popular music genres in Puerto Rico, can be experienced at numerous venues across the island. The lively bars and clubs of San Juan, such as La Placita de Santurce and Nuyorican Café, showcase local salsa bands and offer visitors an authentic taste of Puerto Rican nightlife. Dancing to the infectious rhythms of salsa creates an unforgettable experience for both locals and tourists.

Theater and performing arts also thrive in Puerto Rico, with numerous venues hosting captivating shows throughout the year. The historic Teatro Tapia in San Juan, established in 1832, is a cultural landmark that presents a diverse range of theatrical productions, including plays, musicals, and ballets. The theater's grand architecture adds to the enchantment of the performances, providing a unique and memorable experience for theater enthusiasts.

Puerto Rico is also home to vibrant festivals and events that celebrate the island's rich cultural heritage. The San Sebastián Street Festival, held annually in Old San Juan, is a renowned event that attracts thousands of visitors. This four-day extravaganza features live music, traditional food, arts and crafts, and a festive atmosphere that embodies the spirit of Puerto Rican culture.

For those seeking outdoor entertainment, Puerto Rico's natural beauty provides a plethora of options. The island boasts stunning beaches, lush rainforests, and picturesque landscapes, offering opportunities for activities such as snorkeling, hiking, and zip-lining. Places like El Yunque National Forest and Culebra Island are popular destinations for nature lovers and adventure seekers.

Additionally, Puerto Rico has a thriving culinary scene that tantalizes taste buds with its fusion of traditional flavors and international influences. From local food trucks serving Puerto Rican delicacies to upscale restaurants offering innovative cuisine, the island offers a diverse range of dining options to satisfy every palate.

Puerto Rico offers a captivating blend of shopping and entertainment experiences that cater to diverse interests and preferences. Whether you are a shopaholic looking for the latest fashion trends or a culture enthusiast seeking live music and theatrical performances, Puerto Rico has something for everyone. From modern shopping malls to traditional markets, from lively salsa clubs to theater productions, the island provides a vibrant and immersive experience that showcases its rich cultural heritage. With its natural beauty, culinary delights, and a warm and welcoming atmosphere, Puerto Rico truly stands out as a premier destination for both shopping and entertainment.

DINING AND NIGHTLIFE

Apart from its stunning beaches and rich cultural heritage, Puerto Rico also offers an exciting dining and nightlife scene. From traditional Puerto Rican cuisine to international flavors and a range of entertainment options, the island caters to a wide array of tastes and preferences.here, we will explore the dining and nightlife experiences in Puerto Rico, highlighting the various culinary delights and entertainment venues that make it a must-visit destination.

Dining in Puerto Rico:

Puerto Rican cuisine is a fusion of indigenous Taíno, Spanish, African, and American influences, resulting in a unique culinary tapestry. One of the most popular dishes is mofongo, made from mashed plantains and typically served with meat or seafood. Mofongo can be found in many local restaurants and is a must-try for visitors. Other traditional dishes include arroz con gandules (rice with pigeon peas), lechón asado (roast pork), and tostones (fried plantains). Many restaurants also offer a variety of seafood options, given Puerto Rico's abundant coastal resources.

Old San Juan, the historic district of Puerto Rico's capital city, is a culinary hub. Its cobblestone streets are lined with charming restaurants and cafes offering a range of cuisines. You can find anything from traditional Puerto Rican fare to international flavors, including Spanish, Italian, Mexican, and Asian cuisines. Popular spots like Raíces, Café Puerto Rico, and La Mallorca are renowned for their authentic Puerto Rican dishes and warm hospitality. Additionally, the vibrant neighborhood of Condado in San Juan boasts numerous trendy restaurants and rooftop bars, providing a chic and modern dining experience.

Beyond San Juan, Puerto Rico's culinary scene extends to various regions of the island. In Ponce, the island's second-largest city, you'll find a mix of local and international flavors. The La Guancha Boardwalk offers a unique dining experience with its selection of kiosks serving fresh seafood and Puerto Rican street food. In the western town of Mayagüez, you can enjoy a blend of Puerto Rican and Caribbean cuisines. The popular Calle Méndez Vigo is home to numerous restaurants and cafes, where you can indulge in local delicacies and enjoy the town's vibrant atmosphere.

For those seeking a farm-to-table experience, the lush central mountain region of Puerto Rico is a treasure trove of organic farms and local produce. The town of Orocovis, known as the "Heart of Puerto Rico," is famous for its coffee plantations and traditional cuisine. Visitors can participate in coffee tours, sample local dishes, and enjoy breathtaking mountain views while savoring the flavors of the land.

Nightlife in Puerto Rico:

When the sun sets, Puerto Rico comes alive with its vibrant nightlife. Whether you prefer relaxed beachfront bars, trendy nightclubs, or lively music venues, the island offers something for everyone.

Old San Juan is not only known for its historical charm but also its lively nightlife. The streets come alive with music, laughter, and the clinking of glasses as locals and tourists gather to enjoy the evening. Calle San Sebastián is particularly famous for its annual festival in January, but it also boasts a vibrant bar scene year-round. La Factoría, a renowned cocktail bar, has gained international recognition for its creative mixology and lively atmosphere. Additionally, Nuyorican Café and El Batey are popular spots for live music and a taste of the local music scene.

In the Condado neighborhood of San Juan, you'll find upscale lounges and trendy nightclubs that attract both locals and visitors. La Placita de Santurce is another must-visit nightlife destination, featuring a plaza surrounded by bars and restaurants. On weekends, the plaza transforms into a bustling street party with live music, dancing, and a lively atmosphere that lasts well into the early hours of the morning.

Outside of San Juan, Puerto Rico's towns and beachfront areas also offer exciting nightlife options. In Rincon, a popular surfing destination on the western coast, you can find laid-back beach bars where you can sip cocktails while watching the sunset. Isla Verde, a beachfront neighborhood near San Juan, is renowned for its luxury hotels and casinos, providing a glamorous nightlife experience. Furthermore, towns like Ponce and Mayagüez offer a more relaxed and authentic Puerto Rican nightlife, with bars and lounges where you can enjoy live music and mingle with the locals.

Dining and nightlife in Puerto Rico offer a delightful fusion of flavors and entertainment. The island's culinary scene reflects its rich cultural heritage, with traditional Puerto Rican dishes taking center stage. From the vibrant streets of Old San Juan to the lively beachfront areas and charming towns, Puerto Rico's dining options cater to a diverse range of tastes. The nightlife in Puerto Rico is equally exciting, with a mix of bars, clubs, and live music venues that ensure memorable evenings for visitors. Whether you're seeking a taste of authentic Puerto Rican cuisine or looking to dance the night away, Puerto Rico is a destination that promises an unforgettable dining and nightlife experience.

CHAPTER THREE

EXPLORING THE REGIONS

EASTERN PUERTO RICO

The eastern part of Puerto Rico is a captivating destination that offers visitors a blend of natural wonders, historical sites, and cultural experiences. From stunning beaches to lush rainforests, this region has something to offer every traveler. In this section, we will explore the highlights of the eastern part of Puerto Rico and provide recommendations for an unforgettable visit.

One of the main attractions in the eastern part of Puerto Rico is El Yunque National Forest. As the only tropical rainforest in the United States National Forest System, El Yunque is a paradise for nature lovers. The forest boasts an incredible diversity of flora and fauna, including exotic plants, colorful orchids, and various bird species. Visitors can explore its trails, visit picturesque waterfalls such as La Mina Falls, and enjoy breathtaking views from the Yokahu Observation Tower. The experience of hiking through El Yunque's dense foliage and listening to the sounds of nature is truly enchanting.

For those seeking a beach getaway, the eastern coast of Puerto Rico has several stunning options. Luquillo Beach, located just a short drive from El Yunque, is known for its calm turquoise waters and palm-fringed shores. It offers an ideal setting for swimming, sunbathing, and picnicking. Adjacent to Luquillo Beach is the famous Balneario Monserrate, a Blue Flag beach with excellent amenities including changing facilities, showers, and food kiosks. Its wide stretch of golden sand and gentle waves make it perfect for families.

Another must-visit beach in the area is Seven Seas Beach in Fajardo. It is renowned for its crystal-clear waters, vibrant coral reefs, and diverse marine life. Snorkeling and diving enthusiasts will be thrilled to explore the underwater wonders of this coastal paradise. If you're looking for more adventure, you can also take a boat excursion from Fajardo to the nearby islands of Vieques and Culebra, which boast some of the most beautiful beaches in the Caribbean.

The eastern part of Puerto Rico also offers a rich cultural experience. In the town of Humacao, visitors can explore the Casa Roig Museum, a beautifully preserved 1920s mansion that showcases Puerto Rican art and artifacts. Nearby, in the town of Naguabo, you'll find the Malecón de Naguabo, a scenic waterfront boardwalk dotted with restaurants and cafes. It's an excellent place to sample traditional Puerto Rican cuisine and savor fresh seafood while enjoying stunning ocean views.

History enthusiasts shouldn't miss a visit to the city of Ponce, located on the southern coast of the eastern region. Ponce is known as the "Pearl of the South" and is home to numerous architectural gems. The historic downtown area, known as Ponce Centro, features grand Spanish colonial buildings, including the iconic Parque de Bombas, a red-and-black striped firehouse turned museum. The Ponce Museum of Art is another highlight, boasting an impressive collection of European and Puerto Rican artwork.

The eastern part of Puerto Rico is also a gateway to the beautiful islands of Vieques and Culebra. These islands are famous for their pristine beaches, such as Flamenco Beach in Culebra, which has been ranked among the top beaches in the world. Vieques offers the unique opportunity to witness the mesmerizing phenomenon of bioluminescent bays. Mosquito Bay, in particular, is renowned for its bioluminescent organisms that create a stunning glow in the water at night. Kayaking through the bay is an unforgettable experience that allows you to immerse yourself in nature's magical light show.

The eastern part of Puerto Rico is a captivating destination that offers a diverse range of attractions for visitors. From the natural wonders of El Yunque National Forest and its enchanting waterfalls to the pristine beaches of Luquillo, Fajardo, and the nearby islands of Vieques and Culebra, this region has something for everyone. Add to that the rich cultural experiences found in towns like Humacao and Ponce, and you have a recipe for an unforgettable trip. Whether you're seeking adventure, relaxation, or a blend of both, the eastern part of Puerto Rico is sure to leave a lasting impression on every visitor.

WESTERN PUERTO RICO

While the entire island is a treasure trove of experiences, the western part of Puerto Rico holds a special charm that captivates visitors. From stunning beaches and lush forests to historical sites and charming towns, this region is a delightful haven waiting to be explored. In this guide, we will take you on a journey through the Western part of Puerto Rico, unveiling its hidden gems and highlighting the unique experiences it has to offer.

Nestled on the western coast, Rincon is a popular destination for surfers and beach enthusiasts. Known as the "Surfing Capital of the Caribbean," Rincon boasts some of the best waves in the region, attracting surfers from around the world. Its picturesque beaches, such as Domes Beach and Sandy Beach, provide the perfect backdrop for sunbathing, swimming, and water sports. Visitors can also indulge in fresh seafood at local restaurants and soak in breathtaking sunsets from the famous Rincon Lighthouse.

For nature lovers, the nearby El Yunque National Forest is a must-visit destination. As the only tropical rainforest in the U.S. National Forest

System, El Yunque is a paradise of lush greenery, cascading waterfalls, and diverse wildlife. Hiking trails like La Mina and Big Tree Trail offer the opportunity to explore the forest's beauty up close. The Yokahu Tower provides a panoramic view of the surrounding landscapes, immersing visitors in the magnificence of nature.

Continuing our journey, the coastal town of Aguadilla offers a blend of natural wonders and historical landmarks. Crash Boat Beach, with its crystal-clear turquoise waters and vibrant marine life, is a snorkeler's paradise. Visitors can also witness the awe-inspiring natural phenomenon at the Survival Beach Caves, where the crashing waves have sculpted stunning rock formations. For history enthusiasts, exploring the ruins of the Spanish Aguadilla Lighthouse or the picturesque San Francisco de Asis Church is a fascinating experience.

Further south lies Mayaguez, Puerto Rico's fifth-largest city and a cultural hub. The city's historic center, Plaza Colón, is adorned with stunning architecture, fountains, and sculptures, providing a picturesque setting for leisurely strolls. The Mayaguez Zoo, known for its conservation efforts, is home to a diverse range of animal species, offering an educational and entertaining experience for visitors of all ages. Additionally, the University of Puerto Rico's Mayaguez Campus, known for its beautiful botanical gardens, is worth a visit for those seeking a tranquil escape.

A short drive from Mayaguez brings you to Cabo Rojo, a coastal town famous for its stunning beaches and natural wonders. Playa Sucia, often referred to as "La Playuela," enchants visitors with its pristine white sands, crystal-clear waters, and panoramic views of the Lighthouse of Cabo Rojo. Nearby, the Cabo Rojo National Wildlife Refuge shelters an array of migratory birds and native wildlife, making it a haven for birdwatching enthusiasts. The unique pink-hued salt flats of Las Salinas de Cabo Rojo, reminiscent of the famous salt flats in Bolivia, create a surreal landscape that is a photographer's delight.

Another hidden gem in the western region is the town of Isabela. With its laid-back vibe and unspoiled beaches, Isabela offers a tranquil escape from the bustling tourist crowds. Surfers flock to Jobos Beach, known for its consistent waves, while Shacks Beach is a favorite spot for snorkeling and diving. The Guajataca Tunnel, an engineering marvel, is a must-see attraction, as it offers stunning views of the coastline and the crashing waves below.

Venturing further inland, the town of Lares showcases Puerto Rico's rich cultural heritage. Known as the "Cradle of the Puerto Rican Flag," Lares played a significant role in the island's struggle for independence. The Casa Museo de Lares provides insight into the town's history and the events that unfolded during the Grito de Lares uprising. Visitors can also explore the nearby Toro Negro Forest Reserve, which offers breathtaking vistas, hiking trails, and the opportunity to see the stunning waterfall, Salto de Doña Juana.

No visit to the western part of Puerto Rico would be complete without experiencing the flavors of the region. The town of Hormigueros, known as the "Land of the Mascots," is famous for its culinary delights. Indulge in traditional Puerto Rican cuisine, including delectable dishes like mofongo, lechón asado (roast pig), and arroz con gandules (rice with pigeon peas). The food festivals held throughout the year, such as the Mango Festival and the Coffee Festival, offer a fantastic opportunity to savor the local flavors and immerse yourself in the vibrant culture.

The western part of Puerto Rico is a captivating region that offers a diverse range of experiences for visitors. From the world-class surf breaks of Rincon to the natural wonders of Cabo Rojo and the rich history of Mayaguez and Lares, this area has something for everyone. Whether you seek adventure, relaxation, cultural immersion, or simply a taste of paradise, the western part of Puerto Rico is sure to leave you with lasting memories and a desire to return.

SOUTHERN PUERTO RICO

The southern part of Puerto Rico is a vibrant and captivating region that offers visitors a unique blend of natural beauty, cultural heritage, and exciting attractions. From stunning beaches and lush forests to historic landmarks and delicious cuisine, the southern region has something for everyone. In this guide, we will explore the highlights of the southern part of Puerto Rico and provide an in-depth guide for visitors looking to make the most of their trip.

One of the main draws of the southern region is its spectacular coastline, featuring pristine beaches with crystal-clear waters and soft golden sands. Playa Sucia, located in the Cabo Rojo National Wildlife Refuge, is a must-visit beach known for its breathtaking views and dramatic cliffs. The calm waters of Playa Santa in Guánica are perfect for swimming and snorkeling, allowing visitors to explore the colorful underwater world of Puerto Rico. For those seeking a more adventurous experience, the beaches of Parguera offer the opportunity to go kayaking through the mesmerizing bioluminescent bay, where the water glows at night due to the presence of microscopic organisms.

In addition to its stunning beaches, the southern region of Puerto Rico is home to several magnificent natural attractions. The Guánica State Forest, also known as the "Bosque Seco," is a UNESCO-designated biosphere reserve and one of the best-preserved dry forests in the Caribbean. It offers hiking trails that lead visitors through a diverse ecosystem, showcasing unique plant and animal species. The Carite State Forest is another popular destination, featuring picturesque waterfalls, panoramic viewpoints, and picnic areas where visitors can relax and immerse themselves in nature.

For history buffs, the southern region has a rich heritage waiting to be discovered. Ponce, known as the "Pearl of the South," is a charming city with a wealth of architectural treasures. The historic district, Ponce Pueblo, is home to elegant Spanish colonial buildings, including the iconic Parque de Bombas, a vibrant red and black-striped firehouse that now serves as a museum. The Ponce Museum of Art houses an impressive collection of European and Puerto Rican artwork, while the Serralles Castle offers a glimpse into the opulent lifestyle of a sugar baron.

Another historical gem in the southern region is the city of Guayanilla, which boasts a well-preserved Spanish colonial center. Visitors can explore the San Antonio de Padua Church, a beautiful example of 16th-century architecture, and stroll along the picturesque Calle Luna, lined with colorful buildings and quaint shops. The Casa Cautiño Museum provides a glimpse into the lives of Puerto Rican families during the 19th century, with its collection of antiques and period furniture.

Food lovers will find plenty to satisfy their taste buds in the southern region of Puerto Rico. The region's cuisine is a delicious fusion of Spanish, African, and indigenous Taíno flavors. From mouthwatering seafood dishes to hearty stews and traditional snacks, the local gastronomy is a true delight. Make sure to try the famous mofongo, a savory dish made from mashed plantains and filled with a variety of meats or seafood. Don't miss the opportunity to sample some local delicacies at the numerous food stalls and family-owned restaurants scattered throughout the region.

For those seeking a vibrant nightlife, the southern region has a lively scene, particularly in the city of Ponce. The La Guancha Boardwalk is a popular gathering spot where visitors can enjoy live music, dance, and indulge in delicious street food. Ponce also hosts various festivals throughout the year, such as the Carnaval de Ponce and the Ponce Jazz Festival, offering visitors a chance to immerse themselves in the local culture and experience the infectious rhythms of Puerto Rican music.

When planning a visit to the southern region of Puerto Rico, it's essential to consider the best time to go. The region enjoys a tropical climate, with warm temperatures year-round. The peak tourist season is typically during the winter months, from December to April when the weather is pleasant and dry. However, visiting during the offseason can be equally rewarding, as it offers a quieter and more relaxed experience, with the added benefit of lower prices and fewer crowds.

In terms of accommodation, the southern region offers a wide range of options to suit every budget and preference. From luxury beachfront resorts to cozy guesthouses and boutique hotels, there are plenty of choices available. Ponce and Guánica are two convenient base locations for exploring the region, with a good selection of accommodations and easy access to the main attractions.

The southern part of Puerto Rico is a captivating destination that offers a diverse array of attractions for visitors. Whether you're seeking sun-soaked beaches, breathtaking natural wonders, fascinating historical sites, or a vibrant cultural experience, this region has it all. With its warm hospitality, delectable cuisine, and stunning landscapes, the southern region of Puerto Rico is sure to leave a lasting impression on every visitor. So, pack your bags, embark on an adventure, and discover the hidden treasures of this enchanting corner of the Caribbean.

NORTHERN PUERTO RICO

The northern part of Puerto Rico, in particular, offers an array of attractions and experiences that make it a paradise for visitors. From stunning beaches and lush rainforests to historic sites and lively cities, this region is a treasure trove waiting to be discovered. In this article, we will delve into the wonders of the northern part of Puerto Rico, showcasing its top destinations and highlighting the unique features that make it a must-visit for travelers.

San Juan, the capital city of Puerto Rico, is the gateway to the northern region. Steeped in history, San Juan is home to Old San Juan, a UNESCO World Heritage site renowned for its charming colonial architecture and cobblestone streets. Visitors can explore the imposing forts of Castillo

San Felipe del Morro and Castillo San Cristobal, which stand as testaments to the city's military past. The city's vibrant energy is best experienced in the colorful streets of La Calle San Sebastian, where locals and tourists come together to celebrate during the annual San Sebastian Street Festival.

Beyond the historical charm of San Juan, the northern coast of Puerto Rico offers an abundance of stunning beaches. The coastal towns of Dorado, Vega Baja, and Manatí are known for their pristine shores and crystal-clear waters. Dorado, in particular, boasts luxurious resorts and championship golf courses, making it an ideal destination for both relaxation and recreation. Visitors can bask in the sun on the golden sands of Balneario de Dorado or indulge in water sports such as snorkeling, diving, and kayaking.

Continuing along the northern coast, the town of Arecibo captivates with its natural wonders. The Arecibo Observatory, once the world's largest single-dish radio telescope, offers a unique opportunity to gaze at the stars and unravel the mysteries of the universe. Nature enthusiasts will find solace in the nearby Cambalache Forest

Reserve, a haven of biodiversity with hiking trails that wind through lush landscapes, providing glimpses of native flora and fauna.

For those seeking a more adventurous experience, the El Yunque National Forest beckons. Located in the eastern part of the region, El Yunque is the only tropical rainforest in the United States National Forest System. Hiking trails crisscross the forest, leading visitors to cascading waterfalls, panoramic viewpoints, and exotic wildlife. The exhilarating climb to the top of El Yunque Peak rewards adventurers with breathtaking vistas of the lush forest canopy and the azure Caribbean Sea beyond.

The northern part of Puerto Rico also offers a taste of local culture and traditions. In the town of Hatillo, visitors can witness the colorful Hatillo Masks Festival, held every December. The festival showcases the town's Afro-Caribbean heritage, with participants donning vibrant masks and costumes as they dance through the streets to the rhythm of traditional music. Similarly, the coastal town of Vega Alta hosts the Festival del Tinglar, celebrating the nesting season of the leatherback turtle, one of the world's largest marine reptiles.

As the sun sets over the northern coast, visitors can explore the vibrant nightlife of Puerto Rico. The lively town of Isla Verde, just east of San Juan, boasts a bustling strip of bars, clubs, and casinos, where visitors can dance the night away to pulsating rhythms of salsa and reggaeton. For a more laid-back evening, the charming town of Aguadilla offers beachside bars and restaurants, where visitors can enjoy a cocktail while savoring the sunset.

The northern part of Puerto Rico is a veritable paradise for visitors, offering a diverse range of attractions and experiences. From the historical charm of Old San Juan to the pristine beaches of Dorado and the natural wonders of El Yunque, this region provides an immersive journey through Puerto Rico's rich culture and breathtaking landscapes. Whether you seek relaxation, adventure, or a vibrant nightlife, the northern part of Puerto Rico promises to leave a lasting impression on every traveler lucky enough to explore its wonders. So pack your bags, soak up the sun, and let the enchantment of Puerto Rico's northern coast unfold before your eyes.

OFFSHORE ISLANDS AND CAYS

Puerto Rico, an enchanting island in the Caribbean, offers visitors a plethora of natural wonders and cultural delights. Beyond the main island's bustling cities and pristine beaches, lie a collection of offshore islands and cays that are waiting to be discovered. These hidden gems provide an idyllic escape for travelers seeking a more secluded and authentic Caribbean experience. In this guide, we will embark on a journey to explore some of Puerto Rico's most alluring offshore islands and cays, uncovering their unique attractions, natural beauty, and recreational opportunities.

1. Vieques

Located just 8 miles off the eastern coast of mainland Puerto Rico, Vieques is renowned for its pristine beaches, crystal-clear waters, and unspoiled landscapes. The island's most famous attraction is Mosquito Bay, one of the world's brightest bioluminescent bays, where visitors can witness the magical glow of microscopic organisms known as dinoflagellates. Vieques also boasts other picturesque beaches like Sun Bay and Navío Beach, perfect for swimming, snorkeling, and sunbathing. Nature lovers can explore the Vieques National Wildlife Refuge, a protected area home to diverse ecosystems, including mangrove forests and salt flats. The island also offers opportunities for horseback riding, kayaking, and hiking, allowing visitors to immerse themselves in its natural wonders.

2. Culebra

Situated 17 miles east of mainland Puerto Rico, Culebra is a paradise for beach enthusiasts and underwater explorers. Flamenco Beach, often ranked among the world's best beaches, enchants visitors with its powdery white sands and crystal-clear turquoise waters. Snorkeling and scuba diving in Culebra's coral reefs reveal vibrant marine life, including colorful fish and sea turtles. For a tranquil getaway, visitors can head to Zoni Beach or Tamarindo Beach, where they can unwind amidst unspoiled natural beauty. Culebra's Culebrita Island, a small uninhabited island nearby, features a picturesque lighthouse, tidal pools, and a stunning beach known as Tortuga Bay. Exploring Culebra's rustic charm, visitors can also indulge in fresh seafood at local eateries or embark on a kayak adventure to the secluded Luis Peña Cay.

3. Mona Island

Located roughly halfway between Puerto Rico and the Dominican Republic, Mona Island is a nature lover's paradise. Protected as a nature reserve, this uninhabited island offers a unique opportunity to experience untouched wilderness. Mona Island's breathtaking coastline is dotted with secluded beaches, dramatic cliffs, and hidden caves, making it an ideal destination for snorkeling, hiking, and birdwatching. The island's underwater world is teeming with marine life, including colorful coral reefs, tropical fish, and sea turtles. To visit Mona Island, visitors must obtain a permit and either take a guided tour or arrange for private transportation. Due to its protected status, it is crucial to respect the island's fragile ecosystems and leave no trace when exploring its natural wonders.

4. Desecheo Island

Situated 13 miles off the western coast of Puerto Rico, Desecheo Island is a small uninhabited island renowned for its exceptional diving opportunities. Protected as a national wildlife refuge, the island boasts crystal-clear waters, vibrant coral reefs, and an abundance of marine life. Divers can explore breathtaking underwater landscapes and encounter species such as tropical fish, rays, and even sharks. While the island itself is off-limits to visitors to preserve its pristine condition, diving excursions departing from the mainland offer a chance to experience the incredible biodiversity surrounding Desecheo Island.

Puerto Rico's offshore islands and cays provide an enchanting escape for visitors seeking an immersive Caribbean experience. From the bioluminescent wonders of Vieques to the idyllic beaches of Culebra, and the untouched wilderness of Mona Island, each destination offers a unique blend of natural beauty, recreational activities, and cultural heritage. Whether you're exploring underwater realms, sunbathing on pristine shores, or discovering hidden caves and coves, Puerto Rico's offshore islands and cays promise a memorable and rejuvenating adventure. As you plan your visit, remember to respect the delicate ecosystems, obtain necessary permits, and embrace the spirit of responsible travel. Embark on this journey and discover the wonders that await in Puerto Rico's offshore paradise.

CHAPTER FOUR

NATURAL WONDERS OF PUERTO RICO

EL YUNQUE NATIONAL FOREST

Nestled in the breathtaking landscape of Puerto Rico, El Yunque National Forest stands as a tropical paradise teeming with lush greenery, cascading waterfalls, and vibrant wildlife. As the only tropical rainforest in the United States National Forest System, El Yunque offers visitors a unique opportunity to explore and immerse themselves in the natural wonders of the Caribbean. With its rich biodiversity, picturesque hiking trails, and captivating scenery, El Yunque National Forest is a must-visit destination for nature lovers and adventurers alike. In this section, we will delve into the enchanting realm of El Yunque National Forest, providing essential information and highlighting its key attractions and activities, ensuring an unforgettable experience for visitors.

1. Historical and Geographical Overview

1.1 History El Yunque National Forest has a rich historical background, dating back to its establishment in 1876 by the Spanish Crown. Originally designated as a forest reserve, it became a national forest in 1903. Today, it is managed by the United States Forest Service and encompasses an area of approximately 28,000 acres.

1.2 Geographical Features Located in the northeastern part of Puerto Rico, El Yunque National Forest spans the Sierra de Luquillo mountain range. Its highest peak, known as El Toro, stands at 3,494 feet (1,065 meters) above sea level. The forest receives an average annual rainfall of

120 inches (3,000 millimeters), contributing to its incredible biodiversity and the abundance of waterfalls and rivers that adorn its landscape.

2. Biodiversity and Ecology

2.1 Flora El Yunque National Forest is renowned for its diverse plant life, with over 240 tree species, including the emblematic Puerto Rican dwarf forest. The forest's unique topography, combined with the ample rainfall, creates an ideal habitat for ferns, orchids, bromeliads, and countless other epiphytes. Towering tree canopies provide a sanctuary for coquí frogs, an endemic species known for their melodic nocturnal serenades.

2.2 Fauna The forest is home to an array of fascinating creatures, many of which are endemic to Puerto Rico. Among the notable inhabitants are the Puerto Rican parrot, the critically endangered Amazona vittata, and the Puerto Rican tody, a tiny jewel-colored bird. Visitors may also encounter the rare Puerto Rican boa, the elusive coqui tree frog, and an assortment of vibrant butterflies, lizards, and snails.

3. Exploring El Yunque

3.1 Hiking Trails El Yunque National Forest offers an extensive network of well-maintained trails that cater to hikers of all skill levels. The popular La Mina Falls trail takes visitors on a scenic journey to a picturesque waterfall, allowing for refreshing dips in natural pools along the way. The Big Tree Trail provides an opportunity to witness colossal ancient trees, while the Mt. Britton Trail rewards adventurers with panoramic views from its observation tower.

3.2 Waterfall Exploration El Yunque boasts an impressive collection of waterfalls, each with its own unique charm. La Coca Falls, easily accessible from the main road, showcases a magnificent cascade that cascades over a rocky cliff. For a more secluded experience, visitors can embark on a hike to the Juan Diego Falls or the La Mina Falls, where they can revel in the serene beauty of these enchanting natural wonders.

3.3 Visitor Centers and Interpretive Facilities El Portal Visitor Center serves as the gateway to El Yunque National Forest, providing visitors with a wealth of information, exhibits, and educational programs about the forest's ecology and history. The Yokahu Tower, perched on a mountaintop, offers breathtaking views of the surrounding landscape, allowing visitors to appreciate the vastness and beauty of the forest from a unique vantage point.

4. Environmental Preservation and Conservation Efforts

El Yunque National Forest plays a crucial role in preserving Puerto Rico's ecological heritage. The United States Forest Service, in collaboration with local organizations, conducts various initiatives to protect and restore the forest's delicate ecosystems. These efforts include reforestation projects, invasive species management, and monitoring of endangered species. Visitors are encouraged to practice responsible tourism by following designated trails, refraining from littering, and respecting the fragile balance of the forest.

5. Practical Information for Visitors

5.1 Accessibility and Transportation El Yunque National Forest is easily accessible from major cities in Puerto Rico. Visitors can reach the forest by car via Route 191 or by organized tours departing from San Juan. Public transportation options are limited, so having a personal vehicle or joining a guided tour is recommended.

5.2 Best Time to Visit The forest is open year-round, but the best time to visit El Yunque is during the dry season, which typically runs from December to April. The weather is more favorable, with lower chances of rain, and the trails are less slippery.

5.3 Safety Tips While exploring El Yunque, it is essential to stay hydrated, wear appropriate footwear, and use insect repellent. Some trails may be steep or challenging, so it is important to assess your physical fitness and choose trails accordingly. Visitors should also be mindful of changing weather conditions and heed any warnings or advisories issued by park authorities.

El Yunque National Forest in Puerto Rico captivates visitors with its lush landscapes, pristine waterfalls, and captivating biodiversity. From hiking through ancient forests to witnessing breathtaking vistas, the forest offers an immersive experience in nature. By appreciating and respecting this unique ecosystem, visitors contribute to the ongoing conservation efforts and ensure the preservation of this tropical paradise for generations to come. Embark on a journey to El Yunque National Forest, and you will discover a world of natural wonders and create memories that will last a lifetime.

CULEBRA AND VIEQUES ISLANDS

The enchanting islands of Culebra and Vieques in Puerto Rico beckon travelers with their pristine beaches, rich biodiversity, and captivating culture. Despite their relatively small size, these islands offer an abundance of natural wonders and unique experiences that make them a must-visit destination for any traveler seeking tranquility, adventure, and an authentic Caribbean experience. In this guide, we will delve into the captivating beauty, attractions, and cultural treasures of

Culebra and Vieques, painting a vivid picture of what awaits visitors on these remarkable islands.

1. **History and Geography:** Culebra and Vieques have a fascinating history that dates back centuries. Originally inhabited by the Taino people, these islands were later colonized by the Spanish and eventually became part of Puerto Rico. Today, Culebra and Vieques are known for their status as nature reserves and their pivotal role in the military history of Puerto Rico.

Culebra: Culebra, located approximately 17 miles east of the Puerto Rican mainland, is a tiny gem known for its unspoiled beaches and crystal-clear turquoise waters. The island is part of the Culebra Archipelago and boasts a land area of just 11 square miles. Flamenco Beach, consistently ranked among the world's most beautiful beaches, is the crown jewel of Culebra, featuring powdery white sand, swaying palm trees, and vibrant coral reefs.

Apart from Flamenco Beach, Culebra offers an array of stunning beaches, including Zoni Beach, Tamarindo Beach, and Punta Soldado. These secluded stretches of coastline provide a serene escape from the bustle of everyday life, ideal for sunbathing, swimming, snorkeling, and diving. Culebra's underwater world teems with marine life, making it a paradise for snorkelers and scuba divers.

Vieques: Situated about 8 miles east of the Puerto Rican mainland, Vieques is a larger island spanning approximately 52 square miles. Like Culebra, Vieques boasts extraordinary beaches, but it also holds a unique distinction as the home of the Vieques National Wildlife Refuge. This refuge safeguards one of the world's brightest bioluminescent bays, the Mosquito Bay, where microscopic organisms emit an otherworldly blue-green glow in the water.

Vieques offers a range of stunning beaches, each with its own charm and character. Sun Bay, Blue Beach, and Media Luna are among the most popular, boasting pristine sands, gentle waves, and awe-inspiring vistas. Visitors can indulge in various water activities such as kayaking, paddleboarding, and sailing around the island's coastline.

2. **Natural Splendors and Outdoor Activities:**
   Both Culebra and Vieques are characterized

by their unspoiled natural beauty and diverse ecosystems. Exploring the islands' protected areas and engaging in outdoor activities provide visitors with a deeper appreciation for their ecological significance.

Culebra: Culebra's stunning landscapes extend beyond its beaches. The Culebra National Wildlife Refuge encompasses roughly two-thirds of the island and shelters an exceptional variety of flora and fauna. Hiking enthusiasts can traverse the refuge's trails, encountering indigenous plants, migratory birds, and reptiles along the way. The reward at the end of the trail is reaching the magnificent panoramic vistas from the Culebra Peak, the island's highest point.

Snorkeling and diving in Culebra's waters reveal vibrant coral reefs, sea turtles, tropical fish, and even the chance to spot majestic creatures such as dolphins and humpback whales during the migration season. The uninhabited Luis Peña Channel Natural Reserve, located near Culebra, offers exceptional snorkeling and diving opportunities with its abundant marine life.

Vieques: The Vieques National Wildlife Refuge serves as a sanctuary for numerous endangered species and is a hotspot for birdwatching enthusiasts. The refuge's diverse habitats, including mangrove forests, wetlands, and coastal lagoons, harbor an astonishing array of bird species, making it a paradise for nature lovers.

Visiting Mosquito Bay is an otherworldly experience. Kayaking through the bioluminescent bay at night reveals a mesmerizing display of glowing organisms that create a surreal, starlit effect in the water. It is a truly magical encounter with nature that is not to be missed.

3. **Culture and History:** The cultural heritage of Culebra and Vieques reflects the islands' historical significance and the enduring spirit of their residents.

Culebra: Culebra has a rich history intertwined with its military past. Fortifications, such as Fort Conde de Mirasol, are remnants of the Spanish era and offer visitors a glimpse into the island's past. The Culebra Museum, housed within the fort, exhibits artifacts and tells the story of the island's history, from its indigenous roots to the present day.

The annual Culebra Heineken International Regatta draws sailing enthusiasts from around the world, showcasing the island's love for the sea and its vibrant sailing community. The regatta is a vibrant celebration of Culebra's maritime heritage and a fantastic opportunity to experience the island's lively atmosphere.

Vieques: Vieques has a unique cultural blend influenced by its indigenous, Spanish, and Afro-Caribbean roots. The island's small towns, such as Isabel Segunda and Esperanza, provide a glimpse into the local way of life, with colorful houses, lively festivals, and authentic Puerto Rican cuisine.

Vieques is also known for its vibrant art scene, with numerous galleries and workshops showcasing the works of local artists. The island's artistic heritage is on full display during the annual Vieques Art Festival, where visitors can immerse themselves in the creativity and talent of the island's artistic community.

4. **Getting to Culebra and Vieques:** To reach Culebra and Vieques, visitors typically fly into San Juan, Puerto Rico's capital. From there,

they can take a short domestic flight or a ferry to the islands. Flights to Culebra and Vieques are available from the Luis Muñoz Marín International Airport in San Juan, as well as from the smaller regional airports on the mainland.

Ferry services are available from the towns of Fajardo and Ceiba, providing a more budget-friendly option for travelers. However, it's important to check the ferry schedules in advance, as they are subject to change and may be affected by weather conditions.

Culebra and Vieques embody the natural beauty, rich history, and vibrant culture that make Puerto Rico a captivating destination. From their breathtaking beaches and diverse ecosystems to their historical sites and cultural treasures, these islands offer a unique and unforgettable experience for visitors. Whether you seek relaxation on pristine shores, adventure in the great outdoors, or immersion in the local culture, Culebra and Vieques are the perfect Caribbean gems to discover and explore.

GUANICA DRY FOREST RESERVE

Nestled in the southwestern region of Puerto Rico, the Guánica Dry Forest Reserve stands as a captivating ecological gem. Spanning over 2,000 hectares, this tropical dry forest boasts a rich biodiversity and unique ecosystem, making it a must-visit destination for nature enthusiasts and adventure seekers alike. In this guide, we will delve into the wonders of the Guánica Dry Forest Reserve, exploring its natural beauty, recreational activities, and conservation efforts, providing visitors with a comprehensive guide to this extraordinary Puerto Rican treasure.

1. **Overview of the Guánica Dry Forest Reserve:**

   1.1 Location and Accessibility: Situated along the southern coast of Puerto Rico, the Guánica Dry Forest Reserve is easily accessible from major cities such as San Juan and Ponce. Visitors can reach the reserve by car or public transportation, with the journey offering picturesque views of the island's diverse landscapes.

1.2 Ecological Significance: The Guánica Dry Forest Reserve holds great ecological importance as one of the last remaining examples of tropical dry forest in the Caribbean. The unique environmental conditions, characterized by low rainfall and high temperatures, have given rise to a distinct array of flora and fauna that have adapted to survive in this arid habitat. The reserve is home to over 700 species of plants, including cacti, succulents, and endemic species found nowhere else on the island.

2. **Exploring the Guánica Dry Forest Reserve:**

    2.1 Hiking Trails: The reserve offers a network of well-maintained hiking trails that allow visitors to immerse themselves in the natural beauty of the dry forest. From leisurely walks to more challenging treks, there are options for every level of fitness. Trails such as the Bosque Seco Trail and the Coastal Dry Forest Trail offer breathtaking views, opportunities for bird watching, and encounters with unique plant species.

2.2 Birdwatching: The Guánica Dry Forest Reserve is a paradise for birdwatchers, boasting a diverse avian population. Over 100 species of birds have been recorded in the reserve, including the endangered Puerto Rican parrot and the yellow-shouldered blackbird. Visitors can embark on guided birdwatching tours or explore the trails independently to catch glimpses of these magnificent feathered creatures in their natural habitat.

2.3 Snorkeling and Diving: For those seeking aquatic adventures, the nearby coastal areas of the reserve offer excellent opportunities for snorkeling and diving. The crystal-clear waters teem with marine life, vibrant coral reefs, and intriguing underwater rock formations. Snorkelers and divers can explore the underwater world, discovering colorful fish, sea turtles, and other fascinating marine species.

3. Conservation and Environmental Education:

3.1 Preservation Efforts: Recognizing the significance of the Guánica Dry Forest Reserve, various organizations and local authorities have been actively involved in its conservation. Initiatives such as reforestation programs, invasive species control, and habitat restoration projects have helped safeguard the delicate ecosystem and ensure its long-term survival.

3.2 Visitor Education and Interpretive Centers: To enhance visitors' understanding and appreciation of the reserve's ecological importance, interpretive centers and educational facilities have been established within the reserve. These centers provide informative exhibits, guided tours, and educational programs that shed light on the unique characteristics of the Guánica Dry Forest and raise awareness about the need for conservation.

4. **Practical Information for Visitors:**

   4.1 Visitor Facilities: The Guánica Dry Forest Reserve offers a range of visitor facilities, including parking areas, picnic spots, and restroom facilities. It is advisable to bring your own food and water as there are limited dining options within the reserve.

4.2 Weather and Best Time to Visit: The reserve experiences a tropical climate, with warm temperatures and limited rainfall throughout the year. The dry season, from November to April, is generally considered the best time to visit, as it offers pleasant weather for outdoor activities.

4.3 Permits and Guided Tours: To ensure the preservation of the reserve, visitors are required to obtain permits before entering certain sections of the reserve. Guided tours led by knowledgeable local guides are available and highly recommended, as they provide valuable insights into the reserve's natural wonders and enhance the overall visitor experience.

The Guánica Dry Forest Reserve of Puerto Rico is a captivating destination that offers a unique opportunity to explore a tropical dry forest ecosystem. With its diverse flora and fauna, scenic hiking trails, and immersive educational experiences, the reserve presents a natural oasis for visitors seeking to connect with nature and learn about the importance of environmental conservation. A visit to the Guánica Dry Forest Reserve is sure to leave a lasting impression and a deep appreciation for the beauty and fragility of Puerto Rico's natural heritage.

BIOLUMINESCENT BAYS

Nestled in the Caribbean, Puerto Rico is renowned for its stunning beaches, rich culture, and vibrant ecosystems. Among its many natural wonders, the island is home to three extraordinary bioluminescent bays: Mosquito Bay, Laguna Grande, and La Parguera. These captivating bodies of water offer a mesmerizing spectacle, where microscopic organisms known as dinoflagellates illuminate the night, transforming the waters into a magical glow. In this section, we will explore the enchantment of Puerto Rico's bioluminescent bays and provide essential information for visitors seeking to witness this unique phenomenon firsthand.

1. Mosquito Bay: Vieques Island

Located on the small island of Vieques, Mosquito Bay is widely recognized as one of the brightest and most spectacular bioluminescent bays in the world. The bay owes its brilliance to the high concentration of dinoflagellates, specifically Pyrodinium bahamense, that inhabit its waters. These bioluminescent organisms emit a bright blue glow when agitated, creating an otherworldly experience for visitors.

The journey to Mosquito Bay begins with a short ferry ride from the main island of Puerto Rico to Vieques. Once there, guided tours are available, allowing visitors to paddle through the tranquil bay on kayaks or electric-powered boats. The tours provide informative insights into the bay's delicate ecosystem, its historical significance, and the conservation efforts aimed at preserving its natural beauty.

As visitors glide through the bay's dark waters, the movement of their hands or paddle creates a magical trail of blue light, transforming the surroundings into a surreal scene. The experience is truly awe-inspiring, leaving a lasting impression on all who witness it. It is important to note that visitors are encouraged to minimize their impact on the ecosystem by avoiding the use of sunscreen or any chemicals that could harm the delicate organisms.

2. Laguna Grande: Fajardo

Laguna Grande, situated in the coastal town of Fajardo, is another remarkable bioluminescent bay that beckons travelers from around the globe. Filled with the bioluminescent dinoflagellate species known as Pyrodinium bahamense, this bay boasts a mesmerizing display of light and natural beauty.

To access Laguna Grande, visitors can join guided tours that depart from Fajardo. These tours usually include a brief educational session on the unique ecosystem, followed by an exhilarating kayaking adventure into the glowing bay. As the kayak glides through the calm waters, each stroke of the paddle illuminates the surrounding area, revealing an ethereal luminescence that seems to come straight from a fairy tale.

Aside from the captivating bioluminescence, Laguna Grande also offers the opportunity to explore the diverse flora and fauna that call the surrounding mangrove forests their home. These mangroves serve as an important habitat for countless species and contribute to the overall health and balance of the bay's ecosystem. Visitors may witness intriguing creatures such as herons, egrets, and even manatees during their kayaking expedition.

3. La Parguera: Lajas

Situated in the town of Lajas on the southwestern coast of Puerto Rico, La Parguera is a picturesque fishing village known for its stunning bioluminescent bay. The bay owes its luminescence to the dinoflagellate species called Pyrodinium bahamense, similar to the other two bays.

La Parguera offers visitors a unique experience, as the bioluminescent phenomenon is not limited to just one bay but rather an intricate network of mangrove-lined canals. Visitors can embark on guided boat tours or rent small boats to explore these enchanting canals at their own pace. As darkness falls, the water beneath the boats is transformed into a glowing spectacle, illuminating the way and immersing visitors in a magical ambiance.

During the tour, visitors may have the chance to witness the occasional marine life, such as stingrays or nurse sharks, which add to the sense of adventure and wonder. Additionally, the village of La Parguera itself offers a vibrant atmosphere with local restaurants, bars, and accommodations, allowing visitors to fully immerse themselves in the local culture and hospitality.

The bioluminescent bays of Puerto Rico, including Mosquito Bay, Laguna Grande, and La Parguera, offer an unparalleled natural wonder that enchants visitors from near and far. The ethereal glow emitted by the dinoflagellates transforms these bays into breathtaking spectacles, leaving a lasting impression on all who have the privilege to witness them.

Visiting these bioluminescent bays not only provides a once-in-a-lifetime experience but also raises awareness about the importance of environmental conservation. It is crucial for visitors to follow sustainable practices, such as using reef-safe sunscreen and respecting the delicate ecosystems, to ensure the long-term preservation of these natural wonders.

Whether kayaking through the glowing waters of Mosquito Bay, embarking on a magical journey in Laguna Grande, or navigating the intricate canals of La Parguera, visitors to Puerto Rico's bioluminescent bays are guaranteed an extraordinary and unforgettable adventure.

So, plan your trip to Puerto Rico, and prepare to be mesmerized by the magical glow of these bioluminescent bays—truly nature's own spectacular light show.

OUTDOOR ACTIVITIES AND ADVENTURE SPORTS

Puerto Rico serves as a playground for outdoor enthusiasts. From thrilling water sports to awe-inspiring hiking trails and everything in between, this enchanting island paradise caters to adventurers of all ages and interests. In this section, we will explore some of the most exciting outdoor activities and adventure sports that visitors can indulge in while exploring the wonders of Puerto Rico.

1. **Water Sports**

1.1 Surfing: Puerto Rico is renowned for its world-class surfing spots, attracting surfers from around the globe. The northwest coast, particularly Rincon, is hailed as the "Caribbean Pipeline" due to its excellent surf breaks. Beginners can take lessons from experienced instructors, while experienced surfers can challenge themselves on some of the island's more advanced breaks.

1.2 Scuba Diving and Snorkeling: The crystal-clear waters surrounding Puerto Rico offer an underwater paradise for scuba diving and snorkeling enthusiasts. Explore vibrant coral reefs, encounter colorful marine life, and discover fascinating shipwrecks. Popular dive sites include Desecheo Island, Mona Island, and La Parguera Bio Bay.

1.3 Kayaking: Embark on a kayaking adventure through Puerto Rico's scenic waterways, mangroves, and bioluminescent bays. Paddle through the glowing waters of Mosquito Bay in Vieques or Laguna Grande in Fajardo, where microscopic organisms illuminate the water with a mystical blue glow at night.

1.4 Jet Skiing and Parasailing: Experience the thrill of riding a jet ski along Puerto Rico's picturesque coastlines, or soar above the ocean while parasailing. Various rental companies offer equipment and guided tours for those seeking an adrenaline-filled day on the water.

2. **Hiking and Nature Exploration**

2.1 El Yunque National Forest: As the only tropical rainforest in the U.S. National Forest System, El Yunque is a must-visit for nature enthusiasts. Explore its lush trails, encounter cascading waterfalls, and marvel at the diverse flora and fauna. The iconic La Mina Falls and Mount Britton Tower are popular attractions within the forest.

2.2 Caving in Camuy River Cave Park: Discover the underground wonders of Puerto Rico by exploring the Camuy River Cave Park. Take a guided tour through the intricate network of limestone caves, marvel at the stalactites and stalagmites, and witness the breathtaking subterranean beauty.

2.3 Toro Negro Forest Reserve: Located in the central mountains, Toro Negro offers numerous hiking trails that lead to panoramic vistas, including the impressive Cerro de Punta, the highest peak in Puerto Rico. Visitors can also venture to the mesmerizing Charco Azul, a series of natural pools perfect for a refreshing swim.

2.4 Guánica Dry Forest: Explore the unique dry forest ecosystem of Guánica, a UNESCO Biosphere Reserve. Hike the various trails, such as the Bosque Seco trail, and observe rare plant species, migratory birds, and reptiles. The stunning coastline of Guánica also offers opportunities for snorkeling and diving.

3. **Ziplining and Adventure Parks**

3.1 Toro Verde Nature Adventure Park: Located in Orocovis, Toro Verde is home to one of the world's longest ziplines, "The Monster." Soar through the lush mountainside, experiencing an adrenaline rush like no other. The park also offers thrilling suspension bridges, rappelling, and breathtaking views.

3.2 JungleQui Zipline Adventure Park: Situated in El Yunque's foothills, JungleQui offers an exhilarating ziplining experience combined with educational ecological tours. Glide through the treetops, immerse yourself in the natural wonders of the rainforest, and learn about Puerto Rico's diverse ecosystem.

3.3 Aventuras Tierra Adentro: Located in Utuado, this adventure company offers a range of activities including ziplining, rappelling, and cave exploration. Take the "Megazip" to soar above lush valleys or venture into the depths of the Tanamá River caves for an unforgettable underground experience.

From the sun-kissed beaches and azure waters to the lush rainforests and majestic mountains, Puerto Rico captivates visitors with its abundance of outdoor activities and adventure sports. Whether you're an adrenaline junkie seeking heart-pumping thrills or a nature lover craving immersive experiences, Puerto Rico offers something for everyone. Embark on a surfing adventure, dive into vibrant coral reefs, hike through breathtaking landscapes, or conquer zipline courses that take you soaring through the air. The island's unique blend of natural wonders and adrenaline-inducing activities ensures an unforgettable experience that will leave visitors yearning for more. So, pack your sense of adventure and embark on a journey to Puerto Rico, where adrenaline, natural beauty, and unforgettable memories await at every turn.

CHAPTER FIVE

BEACHES AND WATER ACTIVITIES

Puerto Rico, known as the "Island of Enchantment," is a Caribbean paradise that offers visitors an abundance of breathtaking beaches and exciting water activities. With its pristine turquoise waters, powdery white sand, and vibrant marine life, Puerto Rico provides a perfect destination for beach enthusiasts and water sports lovers. In this section, we will delve into the fascinating world of beach and water activities that await visitors in Puerto Rico, offering an unforgettable experience that combines relaxation, adventure, and natural beauty.

1. **Beaches of Puerto Rico:** Puerto Rico boasts an impressive coastline featuring a diverse range of beaches, each with its unique charm and character. Here are some notable beaches that visitors can explore:

a) Flamenco Beach, Culebra Island: Located on the picturesque Culebra Island, Flamenco Beach is consistently ranked as one of the world's top beaches. With its crystal-clear waters and powdery white sand, it offers visitors a true tropical paradise. Snorkeling, swimming, sunbathing, and beachcombing are popular activities here.

b) Luquillo Beach: Situated on the northeastern coast of Puerto Rico, Luquillo Beach is renowned for its palm-fringed shores and gentle waves. This family-friendly beach provides excellent swimming conditions, and visitors can rent chairs, umbrellas, and indulge in delicious local cuisine from the food kiosks along the beach.

c) Crash Boat Beach, Aguadilla: Crash Boat Beach is a hidden gem located in Aguadilla, on the island's northwest coast. This vibrant beach offers a vibrant atmosphere, vibrant atmosphere, and is popular among locals and tourists alike. Visitors can enjoy swimming in its clear waters, cliff jumping, and snorkeling to explore the underwater world.

2. **Water Activities in Puerto Rico:** Beyond the pristine beaches, Puerto Rico offers a wide array of exhilarating water activities. Whether you're a thrill-seeker or prefer a more relaxed experience, there's something

for everyone. Here are some water activities that visitors can enjoy:

a) Snorkeling and Scuba Diving: With its coral reefs, colorful marine life, and shipwrecks, Puerto Rico is a haven for snorkeling and scuba diving enthusiasts. Explore the underwater wonders at La Parguera Natural Reserve, Culebra Island's reefs, or the famous Mona Island, where you can encounter sea turtles, tropical fish, and vibrant coral formations.

b) Kayaking: Puerto Rico's diverse waterways make it an excellent destination for kayaking adventures. Paddle through the mystical bioluminescent bay in Vieques or explore the mangrove forests in the Las Cabezas de San Juan Nature Reserve in Fajardo. These unique experiences provide a close encounter with Puerto Rico's rich natural ecosystems.

c) Surfing: With its consistent waves and warm waters, Puerto Rico is a surfer's paradise. The northwest coast, particularly Rincon, is renowned for its world-class surfing conditions. Beginners can take lessons at various surf schools, while experienced surfers can challenge themselves with the larger swells at spots like Wilderness and Maria's Beach.

d) Jet Skiing and Parasailing: For those seeking an adrenaline rush, jet skiing and parasailing are popular activities in Puerto Rico. Rent a jet ski and cruise along the coast, or soar above the stunning beaches and enjoy panoramic views of the island while parasailing. These activities offer an exhilarating perspective of Puerto Rico's natural beauty.

e) Catamaran and Sailing Tours: Embark on a catamaran or sailing tour to explore Puerto Rico's coastline and nearby islands. Relax on deck, soak up the sun, and enjoy the gentle breeze as you sail through the turquoise waters. Some tours also offer snorkeling opportunities and stops at secluded coves for swimming and beach exploration.

Puerto Rico's beaches and water activities provide an idyllic playground for visitors seeking relaxation, adventure, and natural beauty. From the stunning Flamenco Beach to the exhilarating water sports options, the island offers an unparalleled experience. Whether you prefer lounging on powdery white sands, exploring vibrant coral reefs, or indulging in thrilling water sports, Puerto Rico has it all. Discover the magic of this Caribbean gem, where the warm waters and breathtaking scenery combine to create an unforgettable vacation destination.

TOP BEACHES IN PUERTO RICO

Puerto Rico boasts a stunning coastline adorned with pristine beaches, captivating azure waters, and a vibrant cultural heritage. A U.S. territory, this enchanting island offers a tropical getaway like no other. With an abundance of beaches catering to various preferences, Puerto Rico has become a popular destination for beach lovers around the world. In this section, we will explore the top beaches in Puerto Rico that visitors should not miss.

1. Flamenco Beach, Culebra:

Regarded as one of the most beautiful beaches in the world, Flamenco Beach is a breathtaking gem on the island of Culebra. Its powdery white sand stretches over a mile, inviting visitors to relax and soak up the sun's rays. The crystal-clear turquoise waters provide an ideal spot for swimming, snorkeling, and diving, offering an unparalleled opportunity to explore vibrant coral reefs and marine life.

2. Luquillo Beach, Luquillo:

Located on the northeastern coast, Luquillo Beach offers a blend of natural beauty and amenities. This crescent-shaped beach is protected by a barrier reef, creating calm waters perfect for families and water sports enthusiasts. Shaded by swaying palm trees, the beach offers a range of facilities, including picnic areas, showers, and kiosks serving delectable local cuisine.

3. Crash Boat Beach, Aguadilla:

For those seeking a lively beach scene, Crash Boat Beach in Aguadilla is an ideal choice. Named after a nearby pier used by the military, this picturesque beach offers golden sand and vibrant blue waters. Its popularity stems from its vibrant atmosphere, with locals and tourists alike enjoying swimming, diving, and snorkeling. The beach is also home to numerous food stalls, where visitors can savor authentic Puerto Rican street food.

4. Playa Sucia, Cabo Rojo:

Playa Sucia, located in the southwestern municipality of Cabo Rojo, is a hidden gem that remains unspoiled and secluded. Nestled within a nature reserve, this stunning beach boasts dramatic cliffs, lush vegetation, and panoramic views of the Caribbean Sea. Visitors can indulge in sunbathing, swimming, or exploring the nearby lighthouse, the historic Faro Los Morrillos.

5. Flamenco Beach, Culebra:

The island of Culebra is home to yet another exceptional beach, aptly named Flamenco Beach. Renowned for its pristine beauty and serene ambiance, Flamenco Beach is a haven for nature lovers. The water is exceptionally clear, allowing for excellent snorkeling opportunities, while the beach itself offers mesmerizing sunsets and ample space for relaxation.

6. Playa Buyé, Cabo Rojo:

Playa Buyé, situated on the western coast of Puerto Rico, is a true tropical paradise. This secluded beach enchants visitors with its calm turquoise waters, white sand, and lush green surroundings. The beach is ideal for swimming, kayaking, and snorkeling, and its tranquil atmosphere makes it an excellent spot for a romantic getaway or a peaceful retreat.

7. Isla Verde Beach, Carolina:

Isla Verde Beach, located just minutes away from San Juan, offers a vibrant beach experience paired with modern amenities. This expansive beach features soft golden sand, clear waters, and a lively atmosphere. With a variety of water sports available, visitors can enjoy activities such as jet skiing, parasailing, and banana boat rides. The beach is also dotted with beachfront resorts, restaurants, and casinos, making it a popular choice for vacationers.

8. Playa Flamenco, Culebra:

Another jewel of Culebra, Playa Flamenco, is a captivating beach known for its postcard-perfect beauty. The beach's calm waters are perfect for swimming and snorkeling, and the surrounding hills offer hiking opportunities for those seeking a scenic adventure. Camping facilities are available, allowing visitors to spend the night under the starlit sky, immersing themselves in the island's natural splendor.

SNORKELING AND SCUBA DIVING

Puerto Rico offers visitors a wealth of natural beauty both on land and beneath its crystalline waters. Snorkeling and scuba diving enthusiasts are drawn to the island's vibrant marine ecosystem, teeming with diverse marine life, colorful coral reefs, and fascinating underwater formations. With its warm waters, excellent visibility, and numerous dive sites, Puerto Rico provides an unforgettable experience for both novice and experienced divers alike. In this section, we will explore the breathtaking underwater world of Puerto Rico, highlighting the best spots for snorkeling and scuba diving and discussing the unique marine biodiversity that awaits adventurers.

1. **Snorkeling in Puerto Rico**

1.1 Snorkeling Basics Snorkeling is a popular water activity in Puerto Rico that allows visitors to explore the shallow waters near the coast without the need for extensive training or specialized equipment. Snorkelers can observe the vibrant underwater world, including colorful fish, magnificent coral reefs, and occasional encounters with sea turtles and rays.

1.2 Best Snorkeling Spots in Puerto Rico

 a) **Flamenco Beach, Culebra:** Renowned for its pristine waters and abundant marine life, Flamenco Beach offers snorkelers the opportunity to explore its underwater treasures, such as coral gardens and tropical fish.

b) **Carlos Rosario Beach, Culebra:** Located near Flamenco Beach, Carlos Rosario Beach is another popular snorkeling spot. Its clear waters and diverse marine ecosystem make it an ideal destination for snorkelers of all levels.

c) Tamarindo Beach, Culebra: Tamarindo Beach boasts calm, shallow waters teeming with marine life, making it a fantastic spot for snorkeling. Snorkelers can encounter colorful fish, sea turtles, and even nurse sharks.

d) La Chiva Beach, Vieques: Known for its turquoise waters and pristine beaches, La Chiva Beach offers snorkelers a chance to explore its vibrant coral reefs and encounter a variety of marine species.

2. **Scuba Diving in Puerto Rico**

2.1 Scuba Diving Essentials For those seeking a more immersive underwater experience, scuba diving in Puerto Rico provides an opportunity to delve deeper into the enchanting marine world. Scuba divers can explore reefs, underwater caves, and even shipwrecks, discovering hidden gems beneath the surface.

2.2 Top Scuba Diving Sites in Puerto Rico

a) Mona Island: Situated off Puerto Rico's west coast, Mona Island is a renowned diving destination. Its pristine waters and protected marine reserve offer divers the chance to encounter large schools of fish, sea turtles, dolphins, and even humpback whales during the migration season.

b) Desecheo Island: Located west of Rincon, Desecheo Island is a remote and uninhabited island known for its spectacular dive sites. Divers can explore dramatic underwater cliffs, vibrant coral reefs, and encounter an array of marine life, including sharks, rays, and moray eels.

c) La Parguera Wall, Lajas: La Parguera is a popular diving site famous for its "wall" formation, where divers can explore a vertical drop-off covered in vibrant corals and sponges. Divers may also encounter seahorses, lobsters, and various tropical fish.

d) Vieques Wall, Vieques: The Vieques Wall offers a thrilling diving experience with its dramatic drop-off and diverse marine ecosystem. Divers can explore colorful coral formations, swim through underwater canyons, and spot an abundance of marine life, including eagle rays and reef sharks.

3. Marine Biodiversity and Conservation Efforts

3.1 Biodiversity in Puerto Rico's Waters The waters surrounding Puerto Rico are home to an incredible diversity of marine species. Visitors can marvel at vibrant coral reefs, encounter tropical fish like parrotfish and angelfish, and spot larger creatures like sea turtles, nurse sharks, and even humpback whales during the migration season.

3.2 Conservation Initiatives Recognizing the importance of preserving this unique marine ecosystem, Puerto Rico has implemented various conservation initiatives. The government has established marine reserves and protected areas to safeguard critical habitats and regulate fishing practices. Local organizations also contribute to conservation efforts through educational programs, beach cleanups, and coral reef restoration projects, aiming to ensure the long-term sustainability of Puerto Rico's marine environment.

As visitors revel in the magic of Puerto Rico's marine paradise, it is crucial to embrace sustainable practices and support conservation efforts, ensuring the preservation of this natural treasure for future generations to enjoy. So, grab your snorkel or scuba gear and dive into the adventure of a lifetime in Puerto Rico!

SURFING AND WATER SPORTS

With its consistent waves, diverse marine life, and ideal weather conditions, Puerto Rico has become a mecca for surfers and water sports lovers from around the world. In this guide, we will explore the various surfing and water sports opportunities available for visitors in Puerto Rico, highlighting its top surf spots, popular activities, and the overall experience that awaits adventurous travelers.

Surfing in Puerto Rico:

Puerto Rico boasts an impressive coastline that offers a wide range of surf breaks catering to all levels of surfers, from beginners to seasoned professionals. The island's diverse geography provides an array of surf spots, ensuring there's a wave for everyone.

One of the most famous surf spots in Puerto Rico is Rincón, located on the western coast of the island. Rincón is known for its consistent waves and hosts various international surfing competitions. The winter months, from November to February, bring large swells to Rincón, attracting experienced surfers looking to ride powerful waves. For beginners, Sandy Beach in Rincón provides more forgiving waves, ideal for learning the basics of surfing.

On the northern coast, the town of Aguadilla offers another popular surf destination. Surfers flock to spots like Wilderness and Surfer's Beach, known for their world-class waves and stunning scenery. Aguadilla benefits from consistent swells throughout the year, making it an excellent choice for year-round surfing adventures.

In the metropolitan area of San Juan, visitors can find great waves and a vibrant surf culture. La Ocho and Isla Verde are two popular surf breaks, easily accessible from the city center. These spots attract a mix of locals and tourists, creating a lively atmosphere where surfers can connect and share their passion for the sport.

Water Sports Beyond Surfing:

While surfing takes center stage in Puerto Rico's water sports scene, the island offers a plethora of other exciting activities for visitors seeking adventure on the water.

Stand-Up Paddleboarding (SUP) has gained popularity in recent years, and Puerto Rico offers the perfect conditions for this activity. Whether cruising along calm bays or tackling small waves, SUP enthusiasts can explore the island's scenic coastlines while enjoying a full-body workout.

For those seeking an adrenaline rush, kiteboarding and windsurfing provide exhilarating experiences. The trade winds that grace Puerto Rico's shores make it an ideal destination for these high-flying sports. Places like Piñones, located east of San Juan, and Cabo Rojo on the southwestern coast offer excellent conditions for kiteboarding and windsurfing, with consistent winds and expansive beaches.

Diving and snorkeling enthusiasts will find themselves captivated by Puerto Rico's underwater wonders. The island is home to vibrant coral reefs, mesmerizing marine life, and intriguing shipwrecks. The Spanish Virgin Islands, located just off Puerto Rico's eastern coast, provide exceptional diving opportunities, allowing visitors to explore vibrant reefs teeming with tropical fish and sea turtles.

Culebra and Vieques, two of Puerto Rico's offshore islands, are known for their crystal-clear waters and pristine beaches. Snorkelers can discover the rich biodiversity of the underwater world, observing colorful coral formations and encountering a variety of marine species.

Safety and Sustainability:

While enjoying the thrill of water sports in Puerto Rico, it is essential to prioritize safety and respect for the environment. Visitors should be aware of their skill levels and choose activities that match their capabilities. It is advisable to seek guidance from local surf schools and experienced instructors who can provide valuable insights into the local conditions and ensure a safe and enjoyable experience.

Additionally, environmental conservation is of utmost importance to preserve Puerto Rico's natural beauty. Visitors are encouraged to follow responsible practices such as not touching or damaging coral reefs, properly disposing of waste, and avoiding the use of harmful chemicals in the water. By respecting the environment, visitors can contribute to the long-term sustainability of Puerto Rico's water sports destinations.

visitors are sure to find an unforgettable experience on this enchanting Caribbean island. With its warm hospitality, vibrant culture, and unparalleled natural beauty, Puerto Rico invites travelers to immerse themselves in a world of thrilling water sports and create lifelong memories in this tropical paradise.

SAILING AND BOAT TOURS

Among the many activities available, sailing and boat tours stand out as an exceptional way to immerse oneself in the beauty of Puerto Rico's coastal wonders. Whether you're a seasoned sailor or a curious adventurer, embarking on a sailing journey or joining a boat tour promises an enchanting and memorable experience. In this section, we will delve into the world of sailing and boat tours in Puerto Rico, providing insights into the various options available, popular destinations, and the allure of this maritime adventure.

1. Sailing in Puerto Rico:

Sailing enthusiasts are drawn to Puerto Rico's diverse coastline, abundant with hidden coves, pristine beaches, and turquoise waters. The island's strategic location in the Caribbean makes it an ideal starting point for sailing expeditions to neighboring islands such as Culebra, Vieques, and the Spanish Virgin Islands. Whether you're an experienced sailor or a novice seeking to learn the ropes, there are several options for sailing in Puerto Rico:

a) Bareboat Charters: For experienced sailors, bareboat charters offer the freedom to navigate the Caribbean waters independently. Numerous charter companies operate in Puerto Rico, providing a wide range of sailboats and catamarans for rent. Embarking on a bareboat adventure allows you to explore secluded beaches, snorkel in vibrant coral reefs, and discover the unspoiled beauty of nearby islands at your own pace.

b) Crewed Charters: If you prefer a more relaxed sailing experience, crewed charters are an excellent choice. These charters come with a professional crew that handles all aspects of navigation, allowing you to simply sit back, relax, and soak in the stunning surroundings. Crewed charters often provide additional amenities, such as gourmet meals prepared onboard, ensuring a luxurious and pampered experience.

c) Sailing Lessons: For those seeking to acquire or enhance their sailing skills, Puerto Rico offers various sailing schools and academies. Experienced instructors provide comprehensive lessons, catering to beginners as well as advanced sailors. Taking sailing lessons in Puerto Rico allows you to learn in a picturesque setting while gaining confidence in handling sailboats in different conditions.

2. Boat Tours in Puerto Rico:

Boat tours offer an accessible and engaging way for visitors to explore Puerto Rico's coastal treasures without the need for sailing expertise. Whether you're interested in wildlife encounters, snorkeling adventures, or scenic cruises, there's a boat tour to suit every preference. Here are some popular boat tour options in Puerto Rico:

a) Bioluminescent Bay Tours: Puerto Rico is home to three of the world's bioluminescent bays: Mosquito Bay in Vieques, Laguna Grande in Fajardo, and La Parguera in Lajas. Boat tours to these magical bays provide a captivating experience as the waters come alive with bioluminescent organisms, emitting an ethereal blue glow. Kayaking tours are particularly popular, allowing visitors to paddle through the luminescent waters, creating a mesmerizing spectacle.

b) Snorkeling and Diving Tours: Puerto Rico boasts vibrant coral reefs and an abundance of marine life, making it an ideal destination for snorkeling and diving enthusiasts. Boat tours take visitors to prime snorkeling spots, such as the Luis Peña Marine Reserve in Culebra or Tamarindo Beach in Vieques. These tours often provide snorkeling equipment and knowledgeable guides who can point out the diverse underwater flora and fauna.

c) Island-Hopping Excursions: Puerto Rico's archipelago includes several stunning islands that are easily accessible by boat. Island-hopping tours allow visitors to explore destinations like Culebra, known for its pristine beaches, and Vieques, home to the enchanting Mosquito Bay. These tours offer opportunities for sunbathing, swimming, and exploring the islands' natural wonders, ensuring an unforgettable day of adventure.

d) Coastal Sightseeing Cruises: For those seeking a leisurely experience, coastal sightseeing cruises provide a relaxing way to admire Puerto Rico's scenic beauty. These cruises often take visitors along the picturesque coastline, showcasing stunning cliffs, hidden coves, and lush vegetation. Some tours include stops at secluded beaches, allowing passengers to disembark and enjoy the pristine shores.

3. **Popular Sailing and Boat Tour Destinations in Puerto Rico:**

While Puerto Rico offers a myriad of sailing and boat tour options, there are a few destinations that are particularly renowned for their maritime allure.

Exploring these destinations ensures an immersive experience into Puerto Rico's coastal wonders:

a) San Juan Bay: The capital city of San Juan is a bustling hub that combines history, culture, and natural beauty. Sailing in San Juan Bay offers a unique perspective of the city's iconic landmarks, including the historic forts of El Morro and San Cristobal. Visitors can also enjoy stunning views of the city skyline and the lush landscapes of El Yunque National Forest in the distance.

b) Culebra Island: Known as the "Island of Enchantment," Culebra is a paradise for sailors and nature lovers alike. The island's unspoiled beaches, such as Flamenco Beach and Tamarindo Beach, consistently rank among the world's best. Sailing around Culebra allows you to discover hidden coves, snorkel in crystal-clear waters, and observe the vibrant marine life that thrives in its protected bays.

c) Vieques Island: Just off the eastern coast of Puerto Rico, Vieques beckons visitors with its tranquil beauty and secluded beaches. Sailing to Vieques reveals breathtaking sights, including the famous Mosquito Bay, home to the brightest bioluminescent bay in the world. The island's natural wonders, such as the Vieques National Wildlife Refuge and the pristine beaches of Playa Caracas and Playa Negra, offer an idyllic setting for boat tours and exploration.

d) Fajardo: Located on the northeastern coast of Puerto Rico, Fajardo is a gateway to numerous sailing and boat tour opportunities. The nearby islands of Icacos, Palomino, and Lobos are popular destinations for snorkeling, swimming, and beachcombing. Fajardo is also the starting point for bioluminescent bay tours, allowing visitors to witness the captivating phenomenon firsthand.

There is a world of exploration awaiting those who venture onto the turquoise waters of Puerto Rico. So, set sail, immerse yourself in the Caribbean's beauty, and let the maritime allure of Puerto Rico leave an indelible mark on your journey.

FISHING AND DEEP-SEA EXCURSIONS

Puerto Rico captivates visitors with its unparalleled beauty. One of the most thrilling activities for visitors is fishing and deep-sea excursions, which allow them to explore the abundant marine life surrounding the island. In this section, we will delve into the rich fishing opportunities and deep-sea excursions that make Puerto Rico a paradise for anglers.

1. **Overview of Puerto Rico's Fishing Opportunities:**

Puerto Rico boasts an array of fishing options for both seasoned anglers and beginners alike. The island's diverse waters, including its bays, lagoons, and the deep-sea, provide a wide range of fishing experiences. Here are some of the top fishing spots and techniques:

a. Inshore Fishing: The calm bays, lagoons, and estuaries around Puerto Rico are perfect for inshore fishing. These areas are teeming with species such as tarpon, snook, bonefish, and snapper. Anglers can enjoy fishing from piers, shorelines, or by hiring local guides with small boats.

b. Offshore Fishing: For those seeking more adventurous experiences, offshore fishing in Puerto Rico's deep-sea is an absolute must. The island is home to various big game species, including marlin, sailfish, tuna, mahi-mahi, and wahoo. Charters and fishing excursions are readily available for anglers to explore the open waters and try their luck at landing the catch of a lifetime.

2. **Popular Fishing Destinations:**

a. San Juan: The capital city of Puerto Rico, San Juan, offers a vibrant fishing scene. With its proximity to the Atlantic Ocean, visitors can enjoy both inshore and offshore fishing adventures. The waters off San Juan are known for their trophy-size tarpon, snook, and kingfish. Additionally, the city's marinas provide easy access to deep-sea charters for offshore excursions.

b. Fajardo: Situated on the eastern coast of Puerto Rico, Fajardo is a renowned fishing hub. Its crystal-clear waters house an abundance of game fish, including sailfish, marlin, mahi-mahi, and yellowfin tuna. Fajardo is also famous for its annual fishing tournaments, attracting anglers from around the world.

c. Vieques and Culebra Islands: Just a short boat ride from the mainland, the islands of Vieques and Culebra offer secluded and pristine fishing grounds. These destinations are known for their untouched coral reefs and incredible biodiversity. Anglers can cast their lines for species like barracuda, grouper, and snapper, all while surrounded by the stunning Caribbean scenery.

3. Fishing Charters and Guides:

To make the most of their fishing adventures, visitors can rely on the expertise of local fishing charters and guides. These professionals have extensive knowledge of the area's fishing hotspots, seasonal patterns, and techniques. Whether you're a novice angler or an experienced fisherman, hiring a fishing charter or guide ensures a memorable and successful trip. They provide all the necessary equipment, including rods, reels, bait, and tackle, making it convenient for visitors to immerse themselves in the angling experience.

4. Conservation and Sustainability:

While enjoying the thrill of fishing in Puerto Rico, it is crucial to practice responsible angling and contribute to the conservation of marine ecosystems. Visitors should familiarize themselves with local fishing regulations, such as bag limits, size restrictions, and protected areas. Additionally, catch-and-release practices are encouraged, especially for endangered or threatened species. By preserving the natural resources, visitors can help sustain the fishing industry in Puerto Rico for generations to come.

5. Safety Precautions and Practical Tips:

When embarking on fishing and deep-sea excursions, it's important to prioritize safety. Here are some practical tips to ensure a safe and enjoyable experience:

a. Check weather conditions and consult with local experts before heading out to sea.

 b. Wear appropriate sun protection, including hats, sunglasses, and sunscreen.

c. Stay hydrated and carry ample drinking water.

d. Follow safety instructions provided by fishing charters and guides.

e. Inform someone on land about your fishing plans and estimated return time.

f. Familiarize yourself with emergency procedures and location of safety equipment onboard.

Puerto Rico's fishing opportunities are sure to leave lasting memories. So, grab your fishing gear, set sail on an adventure, and discover the unparalleled beauty of Puerto Rico's waters.

CHAPTER SIX

CULTURAL EXPERIENCES

Puerto Rico's cultural heritage is both diverse and captivating. From historical sites and traditional festivals to mouthwatering cuisine and lively music,

Puerto Rico provides a multitude of opportunities to immerse oneself in its rich culture. In this section, we will explore some of the most notable cultural experiences that visitors can enjoy on the island.

Historical Sites: Puerto Rico is home to several significant historical sites that showcase its colonial past and indigenous heritage. One such site is Old San Juan, a UNESCO World Heritage site that boasts beautifully preserved Spanish colonial architecture. Visitors can wander through its cobblestone streets, marvel at the colorful buildings, and explore iconic landmarks such as El Morro and San Cristobal forts. These forts, built by the Spanish in the 16th century, provide a glimpse into Puerto Rico's strategic importance in the region.

Another historical gem is the city of Ponce, often referred to as the "Pearl of the South." Ponce's historic downtown features stunning neoclassical buildings, including the iconic red and black Parque de Bombas firehouse. The Ponce Museum of Art, with its extensive collection of Puerto Rican and international artwork, is also worth a visit.

Indigenous Heritage: To delve deeper into Puerto Rico's indigenous heritage, visitors can explore the Tibes Indigenous Ceremonial Center. Located in Ponce, this archaeological site provides insights into the lives of the Taíno people, who inhabited the island before the arrival of the Spanish. Visitors can explore ceremonial plazas, view ancient petroglyphs, and learn about the Taíno's cultural practices and beliefs.

Traditional Festivals: Puerto Ricans are known for their vibrant and exuberant festivals, which celebrate everything from religious traditions to agricultural harvests. One of the most famous festivals is the Fiestas de la Calle San Sebastián, held annually in Old San Juan. This four-day extravaganza features live music, traditional dances, artisan crafts, and a culinary feast of local delicacies. It is a fantastic opportunity to experience Puerto Rico's lively spirit and immerse yourself in its music and dance traditions.

Another popular festival is the Ponce Carnival, celebrated in Ponce during the week leading up to Ash Wednesday. Colorful parades, masked characters, and lively music fill the streets as locals and visitors come together to revel in this festive atmosphere. The Vejigantes, a traditional character adorned in a brightly colored mask and costume, is a highlight of the carnival.

Music and Dance: Music is an integral part of Puerto Rican culture, and visitors can experience the island's lively rhythms through various music and dance traditions. Salsa, with its infectious beats, is a genre deeply ingrained in Puerto Rico's identity. Visitors can attend live salsa performances in vibrant venues like La Placita de Santurce in San Juan or explore the rich history of salsa at the Museo de la Salsa in Carolina.

Another iconic Puerto Rican musical genre is Bomba, which originated in African communities during the colonial era. Bomba performances involve drumming, dancing, and call-and-response singing, creating an interactive and energetic atmosphere. Visitors can participate in Bomba workshops or attend live Bomba sessions in towns like Loíza or Santurce.

Cuisine: No cultural exploration is complete without savoring the local cuisine. Puerto Rico offers a delectable array of dishes that combine indigenous, Spanish, and African culinary influences. From succulent roast pork (lechón) to mofongo (a mashed plantain dish), Puerto Rican cuisine tantalizes the taste buds with its bold flavors.

Visitors can indulge in traditional dishes at local eateries called "fondas" or explore the vibrant food scene in towns like Piñones, known for its array of street food stalls. Don't forget to sample the island's national drink, the piña colada, which was invented in Puerto Rico.

Puerto Rico offers a wealth of cultural immersion opportunities. The island's rich history, indigenous heritage, and vibrant traditions make it a truly unique destination that will leave visitors with lifelong memories. So pack your bags, and get ready to explore the enchanting cultural mosaic of Puerto Rico.

FESTIVALS AND EVENTS

One of the best ways to immerse oneself in the captivating spirit of Puerto Rico is by participating in its numerous festivals and events. From colorful parades to lively music and dance celebrations, the island offers a diverse array of cultural, religious, and artistic festivities throughout the year. These are some of the most captivating festivals and events in Puerto Rico that are sure to enthrall visitors.

1. **La Fiesta de la Calle San Sebastián:** Undoubtedly one of the most iconic festivals in Puerto Rico, La Fiesta de la Calle San Sebastián takes place annually in Old San Juan during the third week of January. This four-day extravaganza celebrates the feast day of Saint Sebastian and features vibrant parades, live music performances, traditional food, and craft markets. The streets come alive with joyous revelers, dancing, and colorful costumes, creating an unforgettable experience for locals and tourists alike.

2. **Carnaval de Ponce:** The city of Ponce, also known as the "Pearl of the South," hosts an exuberant carnival every February, drawing crowds from all over the island. With its roots in Spanish and African traditions, the

Carnaval de Ponce features dazzling costumes, lively music, and energetic dance performances known as "plenas." The highlight of the carnival is the "Vejigantes," masked characters representing Puerto Rico's African heritage. The vibrant atmosphere and contagious energy make this festival a must-visit for anyone seeking an authentic cultural experience.

3. **Casals Festival:** The Casals Festival, named after renowned cellist Pablo Casals, is an annual classical music event held in San Juan during February and March. Esteemed international musicians come together to perform symphonies, concertos, and chamber music, enchanting audiences with their extraordinary talent. The festival showcases the island's rich classical music heritage and attracts classical music aficionados from around the world.

4. **Festival de la Danza:** Dance enthusiasts will be captivated by the Festival de la Danza, an event that celebrates Puerto Rico's vibrant dance traditions. Held annually in Ponce in April, the festival features performances by renowned local and international dance companies. From traditional folk dances to

contemporary ballet, visitors can witness the artistic prowess and diverse range of dance forms that Puerto Rico has to offer.

5. **National Puerto Rican Day Parade:** Every June, New York City's vibrant Puerto Rican community commemorates its heritage with the National Puerto Rican Day Parade. This colorful extravaganza showcases Puerto Rican culture, music, dance, and traditional cuisine. Spectators line the streets of Manhattan to witness the festive floats, lively salsa music, and mesmerizing dance performances, creating a vibrant and lively atmosphere.

6. **Festival Casals de Bayamón:** Another significant classical music festival in Puerto Rico is the Festival Casals de Bayamón, held annually in Bayamón. This event pays homage to Pablo Casals and features an impressive lineup of local and international classical musicians. From chamber music recitals to orchestral performances, the festival showcases the island's deep appreciation for classical music.

7. **Heineken JazzFest:** Jazz enthusiasts flock to Puerto Rico for the Heineken JazzFest, an internationally renowned music festival held

in San Juan. This multi-day event in March features performances by acclaimed jazz artists from around the globe. From traditional jazz to fusion and Latin jazz, the festival provides an extraordinary musical experience against the backdrop of the beautiful Caribbean landscape.

8. **Fiestas de la Calle San Sebastián en Hatillo:** The town of Hatillo, located on Puerto Rico's northern coast, celebrates its patron saint, San Sebastian, with the Fiestas de la Calle San Sebastián en Hatillo. Held in January, this festival includes religious processions, traditional music, and lively dance performances. The highlight is the "Santiago Apóstol" tradition, where masked revelers parade through the streets accompanied by lively music and dancing.

9. **Festival de la Máscara:** The Festival de la Máscara is an annual event held in Vejigante, a small town in Loíza, known for its vibrant Afro-Puerto Rican traditions. The festival celebrates the island's African heritage through colorful masks, music, and dance. Visitors can experience the distinctive Vejigante masks, which symbolize the

island's folklore and provide a glimpse into its rich cultural tapestry.

Visitors to Puerto Rico are sure to be captivated by the colorful parades, exuberant dances, and infectious energy that permeate these events. Immerse yourself in the beauty of Puerto Rico's festivals and events and create unforgettable memories that will last a lifetime.

LOCAL CUISINE AND TRADITIONAL DISHES

Puerto Rico, known as the "Island of Enchantment," offers not only breathtaking natural beauty and vibrant culture but also a tantalizing culinary experience. Puerto Rican cuisine is a fusion of indigenous Taíno, Spanish, African, and American influences, resulting in a unique and flavorful gastronomy. For visitors to the island, immersing themselves in the local cuisine is an essential part of the Puerto Rican experience.

1. **Roots and Influences:** Puerto Rican cuisine is deeply rooted in the island's history and the blending of various cultural influences. The indigenous Taíno people introduced staples such as corn, yucca, and sweet potatoes. The arrival of the Spanish brought ingredients like rice, wheat, and olive oil, while African slaves contributed flavors such as plantains, yams, and tropical fruits. Additionally, Puerto Rico's historical ties to the United States have led to the incorporation of American ingredients and culinary techniques.

2. **Mofongo: A Puerto Rican Delicacy:** No exploration of Puerto Rican cuisine is complete without mentioning mofongo, a beloved traditional dish. Mofongo consists of fried green plantains mashed with garlic, salt, and olive oil. It is often filled with succulent meats, such as pork or chicken, and served with a side of flavorful broth. The dish is a testament to the island's African heritage and is widely regarded as a Puerto Rican culinary masterpiece.

3. **Arroz con Gandules: Puerto Rico's National Dish:** Arroz con gandules, or rice with pigeon peas, is considered the national dish of Puerto Rico. This vibrant and aromatic rice dish combines long-grain rice, pigeon peas, sofrito (a flavorful sauce made with tomatoes, onions, garlic, peppers, and herbs), and various spices such as annatto. It is typically served alongside roasted pork, creating a delicious and satisfying meal. Arroz con gandules reflects the island's Spanish and African influences and is a staple on special occasions and family gatherings.

4. **Lechón: A Feast for the Senses:** Lechón, or roasted pig, is a centerpiece of Puerto Rican cuisine and an essential part of festive celebrations. The whole pig is marinated with a mixture of herbs, spices, and bitter orange juice, then slowly roasted on an open fire for several hours until the skin becomes crispy and the meat tender and succulent. The result is a mouthwatering dish that embodies the flavors and traditions of the island. Visitors should not miss the opportunity to taste this iconic Puerto Rican specialty.

5. **Pasteles: A Holiday Delight:** Pasteles are Puerto Rico's version of tamales, made from a dough of grated green plantains, yautía (taro root), and tropical pumpkins, filled with a savory mixture of meat, such as pork or chicken, and wrapped in banana leaves. These delicious parcels are then boiled or steamed until cooked through. Pasteles are a labor-intensive dish typically prepared during the holiday season, where families come together to make large batches, creating a sense of community and celebration.

6. **Tropical Fruits and Beverages:** Puerto Rico's tropical climate is a paradise for fruit lovers, with an abundance of exotic fruits available year-round. Visitors can indulge in refreshing treats like coconuts, mangoes, guavas, passion fruits, and papayas, which are not only delicious but also offer a taste of the island's vibrant biodiversity. Additionally, Puerto Rico boasts a range of traditional beverages, including piña coladas (a sweet cocktail made with pineapple, coconut cream, and rum), morir soñando (a refreshing blend of orange juice, milk, sugar, and vanilla), and coquito (a creamy

coconut-based eggnog flavored with rum and spices), often enjoyed during holidays and special occasions.

Visitors to Puerto Rico have the opportunity to embark on a culinary adventure that reflects the island's rich cultural tapestry. The fusion of indigenous, Spanish, African, and American influences has given rise to a vibrant and diverse culinary landscape. From iconic dishes like mofongo and arroz con gandules to festive delights such as lechón and pasteles, Puerto Rican cuisine offers a tantalizing array of flavors and textures. Exploring the local cuisine allows visitors to not only savor delicious dishes but also gain a deeper understanding of the island's history, traditions, and warm hospitality. So, come and experience the magic of Puerto Rico's gastronomy, where every bite is a journey of flavors and a celebration of its cultural heritage.

COFFEE PLANTATIONS AND TOURS

This section delves into the captivating world of Puerto Rico's coffee plantations and highlights the remarkable coffee tours available, providing an insightful journey for coffee enthusiasts and curious travelers alike.

1. **A Brief History of Coffee in Puerto Rico:** To truly appreciate the significance of coffee plantations in Puerto Rico, it's essential to understand the island's coffee history. Introduced to Puerto Rico in the early 18th century, coffee cultivation quickly became a vital part of the island's agricultural economy. The fertile volcanic soil, ideal altitude, and favorable climate offered optimal conditions for coffee production. Puerto Rican coffee gained international recognition for its exceptional quality, earning the island the nickname "The Bourbon Island of the Caribbean."

2. **Exploring Puerto Rico's Coffee Plantations:**

2.1. Hacienda San Pedro: Situated in the mountains of Jayuya, Hacienda San Pedro is one of Puerto Rico's most renowned coffee plantations. Visitors can embark on a guided tour that offers insights into the coffee production process. From the carefully tended coffee plants to the harvesting and processing methods, guests will gain a comprehensive understanding of the art of coffee making. Additionally, the tour allows visitors to savor freshly brewed coffee and purchase aromatic beans as souvenirs.

2.2. Hacienda Tres Ángeles: Nestled in the picturesque town of Adjuntas, Hacienda Tres Ángeles offers an immersive coffee experience. The plantation's tour takes visitors on a captivating journey through the coffee estate, featuring stunning panoramic views and the chance to engage with the farmers. Guests can witness the intricate steps involved in coffee cultivation, learn about sustainable farming practices, and sample the flavorsome results of their labor.

2.3. Café Gran Batey: Located in the idyllic town of Utuado, Café Gran Batey provides an intimate and educational coffee tour. Visitors can witness the coffee production process from seed to cup, gaining a deeper understanding of the intricate craftsmanship involved. With its commitment to organic farming and fair trade practices, Café Gran Batey exemplifies the island's dedication to sustainable and ethical coffee production.

3. **The Coffee Tour Experience:**

3.1. Harvesting and Processing: Coffee tours in Puerto Rico offer a firsthand experience of coffee harvesting and processing. Visitors can participate in the harvesting process, picking ripe coffee cherries from the trees and learning about the optimal selection criteria. They can then witness the meticulous steps involved in processing, such as pulping, fermenting, drying, and roasting, which all contribute to the unique flavor profiles of Puerto Rican coffee.

3.2. Coffee Tasting: No coffee tour would be complete without a tantalizing coffee tasting session. Visitors have the opportunity to indulge in the flavors of Puerto Rican coffee, sampling various roasts and blends. Expert guides provide insights into the tasting notes, aromas, and brewing methods, enabling visitors to appreciate the nuanced flavors of the island's coffee.

3.3. Cultural and Historical Significance: Coffee tours in Puerto Rico often incorporate the island's rich cultural and historical elements. Alongside the coffee-related activities, visitors can explore the plantation's historical buildings, learn about the cultural heritage of coffee production, and engage with local artisans who showcase traditional crafts. This cultural immersion adds depth to the coffee tour experience, offering a holistic perspective on Puerto Rico's coffee legacy.

4. **Sustainable and Ethical Coffee Production:** Many coffee plantations in Puerto Rico prioritize sustainable and ethical practices. They employ environmentally friendly cultivation methods, promote biodiversity, and prioritize fair trade principles. Coffee tours provide an opportunity to learn about these initiatives and witness firsthand the positive impact of responsible coffee production on the local communities and ecosystems.

5. **Supporting Local Coffee Culture:** By participating in coffee tours and purchasing Puerto Rican coffee, visitors actively support the island's local coffee culture. The revenue generated from these tours and coffee sales contributes to the preservation and growth of Puerto Rico's coffee industry, ensuring its sustainability for future generations.

By engaging with sustainable and ethical coffee production, visitors not only enjoy the sensory delights of Puerto Rican coffee but also contribute to the preservation and growth of the island's coffee industry. So, embark on a journey to Puerto Rico's enchanting coffee plantations and savor the magic of this tropical paradise through the aroma and taste of its world-class coffee.

RUM DISTILLERIES AND TASTINGS

Puerto Rico, known as the "Rum Capital of the World," offers a rich and vibrant experience for rum enthusiasts and visitors alike. With its long-standing history of rum production and diverse range of distilleries, the island presents an ideal destination for those seeking to delve into the world of rum. This section will take you on a journey through the captivating rum distilleries of Puerto Rico, highlighting their unique features and offering insights into the art of rum production. Additionally, we will explore the various rum tasting experiences available, providing you with a comprehensive guide to make the most of your visit.

1. **The History of Rum in Puerto Rico:** Rum production in Puerto Rico dates back to the 16th century when the island's fertile soil proved to be perfect for cultivating sugarcane, a key ingredient in rum production. The Spanish settlers recognized the potential of this Caribbean paradise and established the first rum distillery in the New World in 1520. Since then, rum has become deeply ingrained in Puerto Rican culture, evolving into an iconic symbol of the island's heritage.

2. **The Famous Rum Distilleries of Puerto Rico:**

   a) Bacardi: As one of the most renowned rum brands in the world, Bacardi offers an immersive visitor experience at their facility in Cataño, just outside of San Juan. Visitors can enjoy guided tours of the distillery, witnessing the rum-making process firsthand, exploring the interactive exhibits, and learning about the fascinating history of Bacardi. The highlight of the visit is undoubtedly the rum tasting session, where guests can sample an array of Bacardi's finest rums, including exclusive releases and limited editions.

b) Casa Bacardi Visitor Center: Located in Old San Juan, the Casa Bacardi Visitor Center provides an alternative experience for those seeking a taste of Bacardi's legacy. This historic venue offers guided tours, informative exhibits, and an exceptional rum tasting experience in a beautifully restored building. Visitors can savor a variety of Bacardi rums while enjoying breathtaking views of San Juan Bay.

c) Don Q Distillery: Situated in the town of Ponce, Don Q Distillery is a family-owned establishment dedicated to producing premium Puerto Rican rum. Guided tours take visitors through the distillation process, showcasing the distillery's traditional craftsmanship. The tasting room provides an opportunity to sample Don Q's extensive range of rums, known for their exceptional quality and distinct flavors.

d) Ron del Barrilito Distillery: Nestled in the picturesque hills of Bayamón, the Ron del Barrilito Distillery is known for its iconic rum, aged using a Solera system. Visitors can explore the facility, witness the meticulous aging process, and gain insights into the intricate techniques that contribute to the distinct character of Ron del Barrilito. The tasting session allows guests to appreciate the unique flavors of their exceptional rums.

3. **Exploring Rum Tasting Experiences :**

   a) Mixology Classes: Several rum distilleries in Puerto Rico offer mixology classes, where visitors can learn how to create delicious rum-based cocktails under the guidance of expert mixologists. These interactive sessions allow participants to experiment with different flavors and techniques, gaining insights into the art of crafting exceptional rum cocktails.

b) Rum Tasting Events: Throughout the year, Puerto Rico hosts various rum festivals and tasting events that celebrate the island's rum heritage. These gatherings bring together local and international rum brands, allowing visitors to sample a wide range of rums, attend educational seminars, and engage in lively discussions with industry experts.

c) Rum Pairing Dinners: Many upscale restaurants and resorts in Puerto Rico organize rum pairing dinners, where carefully selected rums are matched with gourmet dishes. These events provide a unique opportunity to explore the nuances of rum flavors and discover the perfect complement for each course, elevating the dining experience to new heights.

d) Distillery Exclusive Releases: Some distilleries offer limited-edition or distillery-exclusive rum releases, providing visitors with a chance to taste unique flavors that are not available elsewhere. These exclusive bottlings showcase the craftsmanship and creativity of the distillers, making them highly sought-after among rum aficionados.

Visiting Puerto Rico's rum distilleries and experiencing their tastings is an unforgettable journey into the heart of rum culture. Whether you're a rum enthusiast, a history buff, or simply a curious traveler, the island's distilleries offer an array of opportunities to explore the rich heritage and flavors of Puerto Rican rum. From the world-famous Bacardi to the boutique craft distilleries like Don Q and Ron del Barrilito, each visit promises an immersive experience filled with educational insights and memorable tastings. So, embark on this rum-filled adventure and let Puerto Rico's rum distilleries enchant your senses with their traditions, flavors, and warm Caribbean hospitality. Salud!

TRADITIONAL ARTS AND CRAFTS

Puerto Rico, a vibrant island located in the Caribbean, is known for its rich cultural heritage and artistic traditions. The arts and crafts of Puerto Rico offer visitors a glimpse into the island's history, customs, and the creativity of its people. From handmade masks and colorful textiles to intricate wood carvings and pottery, Puerto Rican traditional arts and crafts reflect the diverse influences that have shaped the island's cultural identity over the centuries. In this guide, we will explore some of the most notable traditional arts and crafts in Puerto Rico, highlighting their significance and providing recommendations for visitors seeking an authentic cultural experience.

1. **Vejigante Masks:** One of the most recognizable traditional crafts in Puerto Rico is the vejigante mask. These colorful masks, made from papier-mâché, depict fantastical characters with exaggerated features and intricate designs. The vejigante tradition originates from the town of Ponce, where it is celebrated during the annual Carnaval de Ponce. Visitors can witness the artistry of vejigante mask-making at local artisan workshops and even try their hand at creating their own mask under the guidance of skilled artisans.

2. **Santos (Religious Statues):** Santos, or religious statues, hold a special place in Puerto Rican culture. These hand-carved wooden figures depict saints and other religious icons and are often used for private devotional practices. The art of santo-making has been passed down through generations, with each carver adding their unique style and interpretation. Visitors can explore galleries and artisan workshops in towns such as San Juan and Loíza to

witness the intricate craftsmanship involved in creating these sacred works of art.

3. **Mundillo Lace:** Mundillo lace, also known as Puerto Rican bobbin lace, is a delicate and intricate form of lace-making that has been practiced on the island for centuries. The craft was brought to Puerto Rico by Spanish settlers and has evolved into a distinct art form. Skilled artisans create intricate patterns using threads and bobbins, resulting in beautiful lace products such as doilies, tablecloths, and garments. Visitors can observe mundillo lace-making demonstrations or even take part in workshops to learn the techniques involved in this traditional craft.

4. **Hammocks:** Hammocks have been an essential part of Puerto Rican culture for centuries, providing a comfortable and practical sleeping solution in the tropical climate. Traditional Puerto Rican hammocks, known as hamacas, are handwoven using sturdy fibers such as cotton or nylon. Artisans carefully craft these hammocks, paying attention to the weaving pattern and design. Visitors can purchase authentic Puerto Rican hammocks from local markets

or directly from artisans who continue to keep this traditional craft alive.

5. **Taino-inspired Pottery:** The Taino people, the indigenous inhabitants of Puerto Rico, left behind a rich cultural legacy that is still celebrated today. Taino-inspired pottery reflects the ancient Taino civilization's artistic motifs and designs. Skilled artisans create clay vessels and figurines using traditional techniques and natural pigments, resulting in unique and beautiful pieces of art. Visitors can explore galleries and craft fairs to discover Taino-inspired pottery and witness demonstrations of the pottery-making process.

6. **Bomba and Plena Instruments:** Music is an integral part of Puerto Rican culture, and traditional musical instruments hold immense significance. Bomba and plena are two distinct genres of Afro-Puerto Rican music, and the instruments associated with these genres are often handmade. Visitors can find skilled artisans who craft bomba drums, cuá and maraca instruments used in plena, and other traditional musical instruments. Experiencing a live bomba or plena performance while appreciating the

craftsmanship of the instruments adds depth to the cultural immersion.

By supporting these traditional art forms, visitors contribute to the preservation and continuation of Puerto Rico's cultural legacy, ensuring that future generations can also enjoy the beauty and significance of these timeless creations.

CHAPTER SEVEN

FAMILY-FRIENDLY ACTIVITIES

Puerto Rico is a fantastic destination for families seeking memorable experiences. In this section, we will explore a wide range of family-oriented activities and attractions across the island, ensuring that your visit to Puerto Rico is filled with fun and enjoyment.

1. **Discover the Rich History and Culture:**
   Puerto Rico boasts a vibrant history and a unique blend of cultures. A visit to Old San

Juan, a UNESCO World Heritage site, is a must for families. Explore the historic forts of El Morro and San Cristobal, immerse yourself in the cobblestone streets, and visit the captivating museums that depict the island's fascinating past. Engage in interactive exhibits at the Museo del Niño (Children's Museum) in Carolina, where kids can learn while having fun.

2. **Enjoy Pristine Beaches:** Puerto Rico is renowned for its breathtaking beaches. Spend a day at Luquillo Beach, known for its calm waters and family-friendly atmosphere. Explore the underwater wonders of the Caribbean Sea while snorkeling or enjoy a leisurely swim. The stunning Flamenco Beach on Culebra Island is another excellent option, offering white sands and crystal-clear waters. Families can also partake in water sports such as kayaking, paddleboarding, or taking a boat tour to explore nearby islands.

3. **Rainforest Adventures:** Take a family-friendly hike through El Yunque National Forest, the only tropical rainforest in the U.S. National Forest System. Discover the lush flora and fauna, swim in natural pools, and marvel at magnificent waterfalls.

The El Portal Rainforest Center provides educational exhibits and programs to enhance your rainforest experience. Embark on an exhilarating zipline adventure with one of the many canopy tour operators, providing a thrilling yet safe way to explore the rainforest from above.

4. **Exciting Outdoor Activities:** Engage in thrilling outdoor adventures that Puerto Rico offers. Explore the Camuy River Cave Park, home to one of the largest cave networks in the Western Hemisphere. Take a guided tour to witness impressive stalactites, stalagmites, and underground rivers. For families seeking an adrenaline rush, Toro Verde Nature Adventure Park in Orocovis offers the world's longest zipline, "The Beast." Soar through the lush mountainside, providing an unforgettable experience for all ages.

5. **Interact with Wildlife:** Puerto Rico is home to diverse wildlife, and families can engage in activities that offer unique encounters with animals. Visit the Vieques National Wildlife Refuge to witness the magical phenomenon of bioluminescent bays. Kayak through the glowing waters as microscopic organisms

light up the night, creating an otherworldly experience. The San Juan Bay Estuary offers a chance to observe native birds, manatees, and marine life on guided eco-tours.

6. **Explore Family-Oriented Parks:** Take a trip to the Bacardi Rum Factory in Cataño, where families can learn about the island's rum-making heritage through an engaging and interactive tour. Enjoy the beautiful gardens, taste local flavors, and discover the art of cocktail-making (non-alcoholic options available for children). The Parque de las Ciencias (Science Park) in Bayamón provides hands-on exhibits and a planetarium, fostering curiosity and learning in a fun environment.

7. **Indulge in Local Cuisine:** Puerto Rico's culinary scene is a delight for food-loving families. Sample local specialties such as mofongo, tostones, and alcapurrias from street vendors or traditional restaurants. Explore the vibrant Mercado de Santurce, a food market offering a variety of fresh produce, snacks, and traditional dishes. Engage in a family cooking class to learn how to make authentic Puerto Rican dishes

together, allowing you to savor the flavors of the island even after your trip.

Puerto Rico welcomes families with open arms, promising a vacation filled with fun, adventure, and enchantment.

THEME PARKS AND WATER PARKS

Puerto Rico is home to a selection of thrilling theme parks and water parks that promise endless fun and excitement. This section aims to delve into the captivating world of theme parks and water parks in Puerto Rico, highlighting their unique features, attractions, and experiences that make them must-visit destinations for both locals and tourists alike.

1. **El Yunque National Forest:** While not a traditional theme park or water park, El Yunque National Forest is an exceptional natural attraction in Puerto Rico. Located in the northeastern part of the island, El Yunque boasts lush rainforests, mesmerizing

waterfalls, and exhilarating hiking trails. Visitors can immerse themselves in the wonders of nature, exploring the diverse flora and fauna while cooling off in crystal-clear natural pools. El Yunque offers a refreshing and adventurous experience for those seeking an alternative to traditional amusement parks.

2. **Las Cascadas Water Park:** Nestled in Aguadilla, on the island's western coast, Las Cascadas Water Park is a family-friendly destination renowned for its thrilling water slides and refreshing pools. The park features an extensive array of attractions, including wave pools, lazy rivers, tube slides, and body slides, ensuring a day of non-stop entertainment and water-based adventures. From exhilarating high-speed slides to relaxing sunbathing areas, Las Cascadas offers something for everyone, making it a popular choice among visitors of all ages.

3. **Parque de las Ciencias (Science Park):** Located in Bayamon, Parque de las Ciencias is a unique theme park in Puerto Rico that combines education and entertainment. The park aims to foster scientific curiosity and discovery through interactive exhibits,

planetarium shows, and engaging workshops. Visitors can delve into the world of astronomy, physics, biology, and technology, exploring hands-on displays and engaging in educational experiences. Parque de las Ciencias is an excellent choice for families and science enthusiasts looking to have fun while expanding their knowledge.

4. **Carabali Rainforest Park:** For adventure seekers, Carabali Rainforest Park in Luquillo is an ideal destination. This sprawling park offers an array of exciting activities set against the backdrop of the lush rainforest. Visitors can embark on exhilarating horseback rides, explore ATV trails, zip line through the treetops, or enjoy a peaceful walk along nature trails. Carabali Rainforest Park allows visitors to immerse themselves in Puerto Rico's natural beauty while indulging in thrilling outdoor adventures.

5. **Arecibo Water Park:** Situated in the northern town of Arecibo, Arecibo Water Park presents an exciting array of aquatic attractions. The park features a variety of water slides, wave pools, and lazy rivers, offering endless opportunities for excitement and relaxation. Additionally,

Arecibo Water Park boasts an expansive children's area with water play structures, ensuring that younger visitors have a safe and enjoyable experience. The park's tropical surroundings and thrilling water rides make it a popular choice for families and thrill-seekers alike.

6. **Bosque Estatal de Cambalache:** Located in Arecibo, Bosque Estatal de Cambalache is a unique ecological park that combines outdoor activities with environmental education. Visitors can explore nature trails, observe wildlife, and participate in guided tours that offer insights into Puerto Rico's biodiversity and conservation efforts. The park's serene atmosphere and diverse ecosystems make it an excellent choice for nature enthusiasts seeking a tranquil escape.

Puerto Rico's theme parks and water parks offer visitors an unforgettable blend of entertainment, adventure, and natural beauty. Whether you're seeking thrilling water slides, interactive educational experiences, or the serenity of a rainforest, Puerto Rico has it all. From the exhilarating slides of Las Cascadas Water Park to the educational exhibits at Parque de las Ciencias, each destination offers a unique and captivating experience. Embrace the excitement, immerse yourself in Puerto Rico's vibrant culture, and create lasting memories at these enchanting theme parks and water parks.

ZOOS AND WILDLIFE SANCTUARIES

For visitors seeking a deeper connection with nature, the island offers several zoos and wildlife sanctuaries that provide educational and immersive experiences. Here, we will delve into the captivating world of zoos and wildlife sanctuaries in Puerto Rico, highlighting their conservation efforts, diverse animal species, and the opportunities they present for visitors to learn, observe, and appreciate the local fauna.

I. The Importance of Zoos and Wildlife Sanctuaries in Puerto Rico :

A. Conservation and Preservation Efforts:

1. **Protecting Endangered Species:** Zoos and wildlife sanctuaries in Puerto Rico play a crucial role in safeguarding endangered and threatened species by providing a safe habitat and promoting breeding programs.
2. **Environmental Education:** These institutions actively contribute to raising awareness about the importance of biodiversity conservation among both locals and tourists, fostering a sense of responsibility towards the environment.
3. **Research and Rehabilitation:** They serve as research centers, studying animal behavior, habitats, and developing techniques to support the rehabilitation and release of injured or orphaned animals.

II. Zoos in Puerto Rico:

A. Dr. Juan A. Rivero Zoo in Mayagüez:

1. **Overview:** One of Puerto Rico's oldest zoos, it offers a diverse range of native and exotic animals, including primates, reptiles, birds, and mammals.
2. **Key Attractions:** Visitors can encounter the island's iconic coqui frogs, the endangered

Puerto Rican parrot, and various tropical fish species in the aquarium.
3. **Educational Programs:** The zoo hosts interactive exhibits, guided tours, and educational workshops that focus on conservation and wildlife protection.

B. San Juan Wildlife Museum and Zoo:

1. **Overview:** Located in San Juan, the capital city of Puerto Rico, this zoo showcases both native and international animal species.
2. **Highlights:** Visitors can observe tamarins, flamingos, sloths, and other fascinating creatures while strolling through beautifully landscaped enclosures.
3. **Aviary and Butterfly House:** The zoo features an impressive aviary and a butterfly house where visitors can marvel at the colorful winged inhabitants.

C. Mayagüez Mall Tropical Zoo:

1. **Overview:** Nestled within a shopping center, this unique zoo provides an accessible and enjoyable experience for visitors of all ages.

2. **Animal Diversity:** The Mayagüez Mall Tropical Zoo boasts an impressive collection of birds, reptiles, amphibians, and mammals from around the world.
3. **Shows and Presentations:** The zoo offers captivating live shows and informative presentations, allowing visitors to learn about the animals' behaviors and habitats.

III. Wildlife Sanctuaries in Puerto Rico:

A. Caribbean National Forest (El Yunque):

1. **Overview:** El Yunque, a tropical rainforest, offers an immersive experience in Puerto Rico's natural wonders.
2. **Biodiversity:** The forest is home to an astonishing variety of flora and fauna, including the Puerto Rican boa, the coqui frog, and the Puerto Rican parrot.
3. **Hiking Trails and Interpretive Centers:** Visitors can explore hiking trails that lead to mesmerizing waterfalls and viewpoints while learning about the forest's ecology and conservation efforts.

B. Cabo Rojo National Wildlife Refuge:

1. **Overview:** Situated on the southwestern coast, this refuge encompasses diverse ecosystems, including salt flats, mangroves, and coastal forests.
2. **Birdwatching Paradise:** The refuge is renowned for its bird population, attracting avid bird watchers who can spot species such as the West Indian whistling-duck and the American kestrel.
3. **Nature Photography and Interpretive Programs:** The refuge offers opportunities for nature photography and organizes educational programs to deepen visitors' understanding of the local flora and fauna.

C. Vieques National Wildlife Refuge:

1. **Overview:** Located on the island of Vieques, this refuge serves as a haven for various endangered species, including sea turtles and migratory birds.
2. **Bioluminescent Bay:** Visitors can witness the awe-inspiring phenomenon of bioluminescence in the refuge's bioluminescent bay, a result of microorganisms emitting light in the water.

3. **Guided Tours and Beach Exploration:** The refuge provides guided tours, allowing visitors to explore the pristine beaches, observe nesting sea turtles, and learn about the ongoing conservation efforts.

Whether you're a nature enthusiast, an animal lover, or simply seeking an immersive experience in Puerto Rico's vibrant biodiversity, the island's zoos and wildlife sanctuaries offer a wealth of opportunities. From the educational exhibits and interactive programs at the Dr. Juan A. Rivero Zoo and San Juan Wildlife Museum to the captivating rainforest trails of El Yunque and the diverse ecosystems of Cabo Rojo and Vieques National Wildlife Refuges, Puerto Rico provides a haven for both wildlife conservation and nature tourism. By visiting these establishments, not only can you witness fascinating animal species up close but also contribute to their protection and the preservation of Puerto Rico's natural treasures. So, embark on an unforgettable journey into the world of Puerto Rican wildlife and make lasting memories while appreciating the island's remarkable biodiversity.

CHILDREN'S MUSEUMS AND INTERACTIVE CENTERS

Puerto Rico offers visitors a rich cultural experience and a wide range of attractions. Among these attractions are children's museums and interactive centers that provide educational and entertaining experiences for young visitors. These museums and centers are designed to stimulate children's curiosity, encourage learning through play, and foster creativity.

1. **Museo del Niño de Puerto Rico (Puerto Rico Children's Museum):**

Located in the capital city of San Juan, the Museo del Niño de Puerto Rico is a must-visit destination for families with young children. Established in 1993, this museum is dedicated to promoting hands-on learning and imagination through interactive exhibits and engaging programs. Spread across multiple floors, the museum offers a wide range of activities and exhibits that cater to different age groups.

The museum features various themed rooms, such as a mock supermarket where children can learn about shopping and money management, a health clinic that teaches the importance of healthy habits, and a mini-theater for interactive storytelling. Additionally, the museum offers workshops, science shows, and live performances to enhance the learning experience. With its diverse range of exhibits and activities, the Museo del Niño de Puerto Rico provides an immersive and educational experience for children and their families.

2. **Museo de Arte de Puerto Rico (Puerto Rico Museum of Art):**

While not specifically a children's museum, the Museo de Arte de Puerto Rico is an excellent destination for families interested in exposing their children to art and culture. Located in Santurce, San Juan, this museum showcases a vast collection of Puerto Rican art, spanning various periods and artistic styles. The museum also hosts interactive workshops and guided tours designed for children, providing them with an opportunity to explore their creativity and learn about different art forms.

One of the highlights for young visitors is the museum's interactive gallery, where they can engage with hands-on activities inspired by the artwork on display. This interactive space encourages children to express themselves through art and fosters an appreciation for Puerto Rican culture and heritage. By incorporating interactive elements into the museum experience, the Museo de Arte de Puerto Rico offers a unique and enriching visit for families.

3. **Parque de las Ciencias (Park of the Sciences):**

Located in Bayamón, a city in the metropolitan area of San Juan, Parque de las Ciencias is an interactive science center that aims to inspire curiosity and a passion for science among visitors of all ages. The park features a wide range of indoor and outdoor exhibits, making it a perfect destination for families to spend a full day immersed in hands-on learning experiences.

The indoor exhibits cover various scientific disciplines, including physics, biology, astronomy, and robotics. Children can explore topics such as energy, ecology, and the human body through interactive displays and experiments. The park also offers outdoor areas where visitors can learn about agriculture, biodiversity, and renewable energy. With its interactive exhibits, workshops, and science shows, Parque de las Ciencias provides a stimulating and educational experience for children, fostering a love for scientific exploration.

4. Museo del Mar (Maritime Museum):

Located in the historic town of Ponce on the southern coast of Puerto Rico, the Museo del Mar offers an engaging exploration of the island's rich maritime history. The museum showcases a collection of artifacts, models, and interactive exhibits that highlight Puerto Rico's relationship with the sea.

Young visitors can learn about maritime navigation, underwater archaeology, and marine biodiversity through hands-on activities and immersive displays. The museum also features a replica of a Spanish galleon, where children can experience what life was like aboard a ship during the colonial era. The Museo del Mar provides a unique opportunity for children to discover Puerto Rico's maritime heritage and gain insights into the importance of the sea in shaping the island's history.

5. C3TEC (Children's Science and Technology Center):

Situated in Caguas, a city in the central region of Puerto Rico, C3TEC is a state-of-the-art science and technology center that offers interactive exhibits and educational programs for children and young adults. The center aims to spark interest in science, technology, engineering, and mathematics (STEM) fields through hands-on experiences.

C3TEC features a range of exhibits that cover topics such as robotics, renewable energy, virtual reality, and astronomy. Visitors can engage in interactive experiments, build structures, and participate in workshops that encourage critical thinking and problem-solving skills. The center also hosts science camps, competitions, and educational events throughout the year, providing additional opportunities for children to explore the wonders of STEM. C3TEC serves as an excellent resource for young minds interested in science and technology.

Children's museums and interactive centers in Puerto Rico offer a plethora of educational and entertaining experiences for young visitors. From the Museo del Niño de Puerto Rico's immersive and hands-on exhibits to the Museo de Arte de Puerto Rico's interactive gallery, these destinations provide opportunities for children to learn, explore, and create. Parque de las Ciencias offers an exciting journey into the world of science, while the Museo del Mar and C3TEC cater to children's curiosity about maritime history and STEM fields, respectively.

These museums and centers in Puerto Rico emphasize the importance of interactive learning, encouraging children to discover and engage with various subjects in a fun and engaging way. By combining education with entertainment, these destinations create memorable experiences that foster curiosity, creativity, and a lifelong love for learning. Whether you are a local or a visitor to Puerto Rico, these children's museums and interactive centers are must-see attractions that cater to the young minds eager to explore and grow.

OUTDOOR ADVENTURES FOR KIDS

This enchanting island is a haven for kids seeking thrilling and educational experiences in the great outdoors. In this guide, we will explore a range of exhilarating activities and attractions that will keep young explorers engaged and entertained throughout their visit to Puerto Rico.

1. **Beach Excursions:** Puerto Rico boasts over 270 miles of coastline, featuring some of the most breathtaking beaches in the Caribbean. These sandy shores offer countless opportunities for kids to indulge in various water-based activities, including swimming, snorkeling, kayaking, and paddleboarding. Popular family-friendly beaches include Flamenco Beach in Culebra, Luquillo Beach, and Crash Boat Beach in Aguadilla. These pristine locations provide a safe and inviting environment for children to enjoy the sun, sand, and surf.

2. **Exploring El Yunque National Forest:** As the only tropical rainforest in the United States

National Forest System, El Yunque is a must-visit destination for outdoor enthusiasts. This lush expanse of verdant greenery offers an array of kid-friendly hiking trails, such as La Mina Falls Trail and El Angelito Trail. Along these paths, children can witness stunning waterfalls, exotic plant life, and fascinating wildlife. The El Portal Visitor Center provides educational exhibits and interactive displays, allowing kids to learn about the rainforest's unique ecosystem.

3. **Discovering Bioluminescent Bays:** Puerto Rico is home to three bioluminescent bays, where microscopic organisms known as dinoflagellates light up the water with a mystical glow. Kids will be captivated by the otherworldly phenomenon as they kayak or take guided boat tours through these bays. Mosquito Bay in Vieques is renowned as the brightest bioluminescent bay in the world, making it a must-see attraction for families visiting Puerto Rico.

4. **Wildlife Encounters:** The island's diverse ecosystem provides ample opportunities for children to observe and interact with local wildlife. At the Manatee Conservation Center

in Bayamon, kids can learn about the endangered West Indian manatee and even participate in feeding sessions. The Arecibo Observatory's Science and Visitors Center offers an engaging experience where kids can learn about astronomy, space exploration, and even search for extraterrestrial life. The Dr. Juan A. Rivero Zoo in Mayagüez is another fantastic destination, providing a chance for children to see a variety of animal species up close.

5. **Ziplining and Canopy Tours:** For adventure-seeking kids, ziplining and canopy tours offer an exhilarating way to experience Puerto Rico's breathtaking landscapes from above. Several companies provide age-appropriate ziplining experiences, such as ToroVerde Nature Adventure Park in Orocovis. Kids will soar through the air, zipping across canopies and taking in panoramic views of the island's natural beauty.

6. **Water Parks and Amusement Centers:** Puerto Rico features a selection of water parks and amusement centers that are sure to thrill kids of all ages. Facilities like the Coqui Water Park in San Juan and the

Mayaguez Resort and Casino Water Park provide a variety of slides, wave pools, and water play areas for endless fun in the sun. Additionally, attractions like the Mundo Feliz Children's Museum in Caguas offer interactive exhibits, art workshops, and play areas that cater specifically to young visitors.

7. **Horseback Riding Adventures:** Children can embark on unforgettable horseback riding adventures, exploring the island's lush countryside and stunning coastal trails. Various ranches and equestrian centers, such as Carabalí Rainforest Adventure Park in Luquillo, offer guided tours suitable for all ages and skill levels. Kids can enjoy a unique perspective of Puerto Rico's natural beauty while bonding with gentle and well-trained horses.

Puerto Rico's abundant natural wonders provide an ideal setting for kids to engage in outdoor adventures that combine excitement, education, and unforgettable experiences. Whether it's frolicking on pristine beaches, exploring rainforests, discovering bioluminescent bays, encountering wildlife, ziplining through canopies, enjoying water parks, or horseback riding across picturesque landscapes, children will create cherished memories that will last a lifetime. Puerto Rico truly is a paradise for young explorers seeking adventure in the great outdoors.

CHAPTER EIGHT

PRACTICAL INFORMATION

If you're planning a trip to this enchanting island, it's essential to have practical information to ensure a smooth and enjoyable visit. Here are some key aspects such as transportation, currency, language, safety, accommodations, healthcare, and popular attractions in Puerto Rico. Read on to make the most of your time in this remarkable destination.

1. **Transportation:** When traveling to Puerto Rico, most visitors arrive at Luis Muñoz Marín International Airport in San Juan, the capital city. From there, you have several transportation options:

a. Taxis: Official taxis are available at the airport and throughout the island. Make sure to use licensed taxis with meters or agree upon a fare before the journey.

b. Car Rentals: Renting a car is a convenient option for exploring Puerto Rico. International driver's licenses are valid, and major car rental agencies are present on the island.

c. Public Transportation: Public buses (AMA) are available in San Juan and other major cities, offering an economical way to get around. Ride-sharing services like Uber and Lyft are also available.

2. **Currency and Payments:** The official currency of Puerto Rico is the United States dollar (USD). Credit and debit cards are widely accepted, and ATMs can be found throughout the island. It's advisable to carry some cash for smaller establishments that may not accept cards.
3. **Language:** The official languages of Puerto Rico are Spanish and English. English is widely spoken, especially in tourist areas,

hotels, and restaurants. However, learning a few basic Spanish phrases can be helpful when interacting with locals.

4. **Safety:** Puerto Rico is generally a safe destination for visitors. However, it's always wise to exercise common sense and take precautions. Avoid displaying excessive wealth, be cautious of your surroundings, and keep an eye on your belongings, especially in crowded areas. Familiarize yourself with the emergency contact numbers and the location of the nearest police stations and hospitals.

5. **Accommodations:** Puerto Rico offers a wide range of accommodations to suit every budget and preference. From luxurious resorts to cozy guesthouses and budget-friendly hostels, there is something for everyone. Popular areas for tourists include San Juan, Condado, Isla Verde, and Rincón. Make sure to book your accommodations well in advance, especially during peak travel seasons.

6. **Healthcare:** Puerto Rico boasts excellent medical facilities, including hospitals and clinics, with healthcare standards on par with the United States. It's highly recommended

to have travel insurance that covers medical emergencies. If you require prescription medications, ensure you have an ample supply and carry them in their original packaging.

7. **Weather:** Puerto Rico has a tropical climate, with warm temperatures year-round. The peak tourist season is from December to April when the weather is dry and comfortable. However, the off-peak season can offer lower prices and fewer crowds. It's important to stay informed about the weather conditions, especially during hurricane season, which runs from June to November.

USEFUL PHRASES AND LANGUAGE TIPS

When visiting Puerto Rico, it can be helpful to familiarize yourself with some basic Spanish phrases and language tips to enhance your experience on the island. While many locals in Puerto Rico also speak English, using a few key phrases in Spanish can go a long way in establishing a connection with the people and immersing yourself in the culture. In this guide, we will provide you with useful phrases and language tips to make your visit to Puerto Rico even more enjoyable.

Basic Greetings and Polite Expressions:

1. Hola (oh-lah) - Hello
2. Buenos días (bway-nos dee-ahs) - Good morning
3. Buenas tardes (bway-nas tar-des) - Good afternoon
4. Buenas noches (bway-nas noh-ches) - Good evening/night
5. ¿Cómo estás? (koh-moh es-tahs) - How are you?
6. ¿Cómo te llamas? (koh-moh te yah-mas) - What 's your name?
7. Mucho gusto (moo-cho goos-toh) - Nice to meet you
8. Por favor (por fah-vor) - Please
9. Gracias (grah-see-as) - Thank you
10. De nada (deh nah-dah) - You're welcome

Navigating the Island: 11. ¿Dónde está...? (don-deh es-tah) - Where is...?

12. ¿Cuánto cuesta? (kwan-toh kwehs-tah) - How much does it cost?
13. Necesito ayuda (neh-seh-see-toh ah-yoo-dah) - I need help
14. ¿Puede ayudarme, por favor? (pweh-deh ah-yoo-dar-meh, por fah-vor) - Can you help me, please?
15. ¿Dónde puedo encontrar un buen restaurante? (don-deh pweh-do en-kon-trar oon bwen res-tau-ran-teh) - Where can I find a good restaurant?
16. ¿Dónde puedo encontrar un banco? (don-deh pweh-do en-kon-trar oon ban-ko) - Where can I find a bank?
17. Perdón (per-dohn) - Excuse me
18. Disculpe (dees-kool-peh) - I'm sorry

Food and Dining: 19. Quisiera una mesa para dos, por favor (kee-see-eh-rah oo-nah meh-sah pah-rah dohs, por fah-vor) - I would like a table for two, please.

20. ¿Qué recomienda? (keh reh-koh-mee-en-dah) - What do you recommend?

21. La cuenta, por favor (lah kwen-tah, por fah-vor) - The check, please.
22. ¿Dónde puedo probar la comida típica? (don-deh pweh-do proh-bar lah koh-mee-dah tee-pee-kah) - Where can I try typical food?
23. ¿Tiene menú en inglés? (tee-eh-neh meh-noo en een-gles) - Do you have an English menu?

Transportation: 24. ¿Cuánto cuesta un boleto a...? (kwan-toh kwehs-tah oon boh-leh-toh ah...) - How much is a ticket to...?

25. ¿Dónde puedo tomar un taxi? (don-deh pweh-do toh-mar oon tah-xee) - Where can I take a taxi?
26. ¿Cuánto se tarda en llegar a...? (kwan-toh seh tar-dah en yeh-gar ah...) - How long does it take to get to...?
27. ¿A qué hora sale el próximo autobús? (ah keh oh-rah sah-leh el proh-ksee-moh ah-too-boos) - What time does the next bus leave?

Shopping: 28. ¿Cuánto cuesta esto? (kwan-toh kwehs-tah eh-stoh) - How much does this cost?

29. ¿Tiene esto en otro color/talla? (tee-eh-neh eh-stoh en oh-tro koh-lohr/tah-yah) - Do you have this in another color/size?

30. ¿Puedo pagar con tarjeta de crédito? (pweh-doh pah-gar kon tar-heh-tah deh kreh-dee-toh) - Can I pay with a credit card?

31. ¿Dónde puedo encontrar recuerdos? (don-deh pweh-do en-kon-trar reh-kwehr-dos) - Where can I find souvenirs?

General Tips: 32. Es hermoso/a (es ehr-moh-soh/sah) - It's beautiful

33. Me encanta Puerto Rico (meh ehn-kahn-tah pwer-toh ree-koh) - I love Puerto Rico

34. No entiendo (noh ehn-tyen-doh) - I don't understand

35. ¿Habla inglés? (ah-blah een-gles) - Do you speak English?

36. ¿Puede repetir, por favor? (pweh-deh reh-peh-teer, por fah-vor) - Can you repeat that, please?

37. ¡Qué rico! (keh ree-koh) - How delicious!

38. Estoy perdido/a (ehs-toy pehr-dee-doh/dah) - I am lost

39. ¿Dónde puedo encontrar wifi gratuito? (don-deh pweh-do en-kon-trar wee-fee grah-too-ee-toh) - Where can I find free Wi-Fi?
40. ¿Podría recomendarme un buen lugar para visitar? (poh-dree-ah reh-koh-mehn-dar-meh oon bwen loo-gar pah-rah vee-see-tar) - Could you recommend a good place to visit?

Remember, making an effort to communicate in Spanish, even if it's just a few basic phrases, will be appreciated by the locals and can lead to more meaningful interactions during your time in Puerto Rico. Enjoy your visit and have a great time exploring the island's rich culture and vibrant atmosphere!

HEALTH AND MEDICAL FACILITIES

It is crucial to have an understanding of the healthcare system and available medical services in Puerto Rico. This section aims to provide an in-depth overview of health and medical facilities in Puerto Rico, highlighting the accessibility, quality, and resources available for visitors.

1. **Healthcare System in Puerto Rico** : The healthcare system in Puerto Rico is comprehensive and follows a similar structure to the United States. It operates under the jurisdiction of the Puerto Rico Department of Health and is subject to federal laws and regulations. The island has a mix of public and private healthcare providers, ensuring accessibility and quality care for both residents and visitors.

2. **Public Health Infrastructure:** Puerto Rico's public health infrastructure is well-developed and caters to the needs of visitors. The Puerto Rico Department of Health oversees public health initiatives, disease prevention programs, and emergency response systems. They collaborate with local health departments to ensure efficient management of public health services, including vaccinations, health education campaigns, and environmental health regulations.

3. **Private Medical Facilities:** Visitors to Puerto Rico have access to a range of private medical facilities, including hospitals, clinics, and specialized medical centers. These institutions are equipped with modern

technology, qualified medical professionals, and multilingual staff to cater to the diverse needs of international patients. Some prominent private hospitals in Puerto Rico include Ashford Presbyterian Community Hospital, Hospital Pavia Hato Rey, and Hospital San Francisco.

4. **Emergency Medical Services:** In case of emergencies, Puerto Rico provides reliable emergency medical services (EMS). The Puerto Rico Medical Emergency Corps (PREMC) operates a network of ambulances equipped with advanced life support systems, ensuring timely and efficient response to medical emergencies. The PREMC works in collaboration with local hospitals to provide immediate medical care and transport patients to appropriate medical facilities.

5. **Pharmacies and Medication:** Pharmacies in Puerto Rico are easily accessible and well-stocked with a wide range of prescription and over-the-counter medications. Both brand-name and generic medications are available, and pharmacists can provide guidance and advice on medication use. Some pharmacies even

offer 24-hour services, ensuring access to medication at any time. It is advisable for visitors to bring a copy of their prescriptions or a letter from their healthcare provider to facilitate the purchase of medication.

6. **Health Insurance and Travel Coverage:** Before visiting Puerto Rico, it is essential to review your health insurance coverage and ensure it extends to international travel. Visitors should consider purchasing travel insurance that provides comprehensive medical coverage, including emergency medical evacuation. Some insurance providers offer specialized travel medical insurance plans that cater specifically to international travelers.

Visitors are encouraged to familiarize themselves with their health insurance coverage, carry necessary documentation, and take necessary precautions to ensure a safe and healthy experience on the island. With its commitment to healthcare excellence, Puerto Rico stands ready to provide quality medical services and support to all those who visit its shores.

LOCAL CUSTOMS AND ETIQUETTE

When visiting Puerto Rico, it's essential to familiarize yourself with the local customs and etiquette to ensure a respectful and enjoyable experience. This guide aims to provide an overview of the customs, traditions, and etiquette expected from visitors in Puerto Rico.

1. **Greetings and Communication:** Puerto Ricans are warm and friendly people who value personal connections. When greeting someone, a firm handshake and direct eye contact are customary. Additionally, it's common for people to greet each other with a kiss on the cheek among friends and family members. Addressing people using their titles, such as "Señor" (Mr.) or "Señora" (Mrs.), is a sign of respect.

2. **Language:** Spanish is the official language of Puerto Rico, although many locals also speak English, especially in tourist areas. Learning a few basic Spanish phrases will be greatly appreciated by the locals, even if you can communicate in English.

3. **Dress Code:** Puerto Ricans take pride in their appearance and tend to dress more formally

for social occasions. However, casual attire is acceptable in most tourist areas. When visiting religious sites or participating in formal events, it is recommended to dress modestly and conservatively.

4. **Time and Punctuality:** While Puerto Ricans generally have a relaxed approach to time, it is still considered polite to be punctual for business appointments and formal occasions. However, social gatherings and informal events often start later than the scheduled time. It's advisable to inquire about the expected time of arrival or check with locals to avoid any confusion.

5. **Dining Etiquette:** Puerto Rican cuisine is flavorful and diverse, and dining experiences are highly regarded. When invited to someone's home for a meal, it is customary to bring a small gift for the host, such as flowers or a bottle of wine. Puerto Ricans enjoy their meals and appreciate unhurried dining experiences, so it is considered impolite to rush through a meal.

6. **Tipping:** Tipping is customary in Puerto Rico, and service charges are rarely included in the bill. In restaurants, a 15-20% tip is expected for good service. It is also customary to tip

hotel staff, taxi drivers, tour guides, and other service providers. Always check for any service charges before tipping.

7. **Respect for Culture and Religion:** Puerto Ricans have a strong cultural and religious identity. It is essential to respect their traditions and customs. When visiting churches or religious sites, dress modestly and speak softly. Taking photographs may be prohibited in certain areas, so it's advisable to ask for permission beforehand.

8. **Personal Space and Gestures:** Puerto Ricans are generally warm and affectionate, and they often engage in physical contact during conversations. Light touching, such as patting the back or forearm, is common among friends and family. However, it is important to respect personal boundaries and gauge the level of familiarity before engaging in physical contact.

9. **Festivals and Celebrations:** Puerto Rico is renowned for its vibrant festivals and celebrations throughout the year. Visitors are encouraged to participate in these cultural events, such as the San Sebastián Street Festival or the Fiestas de la Calle San Sebastián, with respect and enthusiasm.

Observe local customs, follow instructions from authorities, and embrace the joyous atmosphere.

10. **Environmental Respect:** Puerto Rico's natural beauty is a significant attraction, and it is crucial to be mindful of environmental preservation. Avoid littering, use designated trails in natural areas, and follow any instructions or guidelines provided by park rangers or tour guides.

By familiarizing yourself with the customs and etiquette of Puerto Rico, you can show respect for the local culture and enhance your overall experience as a visitor. Remember to embrace the warmth and hospitality of Puerto Ricans, and be open to new experiences. By following these guidelines, you will forge meaningful connections and create lasting memories on your journey through the captivating island of Puerto Rico.

INTERNET AND COMMUNICATION

In today's interconnected world, reliable internet and effective communication services are essential for travelers, allowing them to stay connected, informed, and make the most of their experience. Puerto Rico offers a variety of internet and communication options to ensure visitors can stay connected throughout their stay. This guide provides a comprehensive overview of the internet and communication landscape in Puerto Rico for visitors, including information on internet access, mobile services, public Wi-Fi availability, and communication etiquette.

1. **Internet Access in Puerto Rico:**

Puerto Rico provides a wide range of options for internet access, ensuring that visitors can stay connected during their visit. Some common methods of accessing the internet in Puerto Rico include:

a. Mobile Data: Major mobile network operators in Puerto Rico offer reliable 4G and 5G connectivity. Visitors can either use their international roaming plans or purchase prepaid SIM cards from local service providers to access the internet on their smartphones, tablets, or other mobile devices.

b. Fixed Broadband: Many hotels, resorts, and vacation rentals in Puerto Rico offer complimentary Wi-Fi access to their guests. Additionally, visitors can find internet cafes and co-working spaces in major cities like San Juan, which provide high-speed internet access for a nominal fee.

c. Public Wi-Fi: Public Wi-Fi hotspots are available in various locations across Puerto Rico, including airports, restaurants, cafes, and shopping centers. While these networks can be convenient, it is advisable to exercise caution and use secure connections to protect personal information.

2. Mobile Services and Providers:

When it comes to mobile services, Puerto Rico boasts several reputable providers, offering excellent coverage and competitive pricing. Some prominent mobile network operators in Puerto Rico include:

a. Claro Puerto Rico: Claro is one of the leading providers in Puerto Rico, offering comprehensive mobile services, including voice, data, and messaging. They provide various prepaid and postpaid plans tailored to different needs.

b. AT&T Puerto Rico: AT&T is a well-known international provider with a significant presence in Puerto Rico. They offer a range of voice, data, and messaging plans for both domestic and international travelers.

c. T-Mobile Puerto Rico: T-Mobile is another major mobile network operator, providing reliable connectivity and competitive pricing options. They offer various plans suitable for short-term visitors or those staying for an extended period.

3. Public Wi-Fi Availability:

Public Wi-Fi hotspots are increasingly prevalent throughout Puerto Rico, making it easier for visitors to access the internet on the go. Some common places where public Wi-Fi is available include:

a. Airports: Major airports in Puerto Rico, such as Luis Muñoz Marín International Airport in San Juan, offer free Wi-Fi services to passengers. This allows travelers to stay connected while waiting for flights or upon arrival.

b. Restaurants and Cafes: Many restaurants, cafes, and fast-food chains in Puerto Rico provide complimentary Wi-Fi access to their customers. This enables visitors to browse the web, check emails, and share their experiences with friends and family.

c. Tourist Attractions: Popular tourist attractions, such as historic sites, museums, and parks, often offer public Wi-Fi hotspots. Visitors can take advantage of these connections to access information, navigate maps, and share their experiences in real-time.

4. Communication Etiquette:

When communicating in Puerto Rico, visitors should be mindful of the local customs and etiquettes. Some key points to keep in mind include:

a. Language: Spanish is the primary language spoken in Puerto Rico. While many locals also speak English, making an effort to learn basic

Spanish phrases and greetings can greatly enhance communication and show respect for the local culture.

b. Greetings: Puerto Ricans value personal connections and often greet each other with a handshake, hug, or kiss on the cheek. Visitors should be open to these warm greetings and reciprocate accordingly.

c. Respectful Communication: Politeness and respect are highly regarded in Puerto Rican culture. Using "por favor" (please) and "gracias" (thank you) while interacting with locals can go a long way in fostering positive communication experiences.

In Puerto Rico, visitors have various options for internet access and communication services to ensure they can stay connected throughout their stay. From mobile data and fixed broadband to public Wi-Fi hotspots, the island offers a range of choices to meet the needs of travelers. By familiarizing themselves with the available options and adhering to local communication etiquette, visitors can make the most of their time in Puerto

Rico while staying connected with their loved ones and the digital world.

ENJOY YOUR TRIP TO PUERTO RICO

AND I HOPE THIS GUIDE WAS HELPFUL

DELZY CARES!

Made in the USA
Thornton, CO
07/24/23 13:07:46

fda8cf4b-6469-4d7e-9a6f-55f34881002aR01